icon

icon

EDITED BY AMY SCHOLDER

THE FEMINIST PRESS
AT THE CITY UNIVERSITY OF NEW YORK
FEMINISTPRESS.ORG

Published in 2014 by the Feminist Press
at the City University of New York
The Graduate Center
365 Fifth Avenue, Suite 5406
New York, NY 10016

feministpress.org

Introduction copyright © 2014 Amy Scholder
Selection and compilation copyright © 2014 Amy Scholder
Individual copyrights retained by contributors.

 This book was made possible thanks to a grant from New York State Council
on the Arts with the support of Governor Andrew Cuomo and the New York
State Legislature.

First printing October 2014

Cover design by Drew Stevens
Text design by Suki Boynton

Library of Congress Cataloging-in-Publication Data
Icon / edited by Amy Scholder.
    pages cm
  ISBN 978-1-55861-866-4 (paperback) — ISBN 978-1-55861-867-1 (ebook)
1. Authors, American—Biography—History and criticism. 2. Women authors, Amer-
ican—20th century—Biography. 3. Women musicians—United States—Biography. 4.
Biography as a literary form. I. Scholder, Amy, editor.
  PS129.I36 2014
  814'.608—dc23

                                                                            2014027419

for evy scholder
in loving memory

CONTENTS

INTRODUCTION
AMY SCHOLDER

On a hot day in June of 1969, I was riding in the backseat of a brown Buick Riviera, going down Interstate 5, moving from San Francisco to Los Angeles with my family. I was six years old. It was the day after Judy Garland died. As the radio announcer reported the tragedy, my mother wept in the front seat, her sense of loss palpable though incomprehensible to my sister and me, who had yet to cathect onto celebrities as loved ones—another kind of family.

We settled into our Encino home, a quiet suburb located close to "town"—what Los Angelenos still call the vast sprawl. Dining at a chic bistro with the promise of star sightings became a family tradition. My parents were pleased with themselves that our standard of living had risen considerably with this move. My father was dedicated to working and making money; my mother became a full-time homemaker. Stacy, my older sister, threw herself into a competitive third-grader's social world, while I stayed at home with my mom, shy and awkward around other kids. We sat by the pool every day that first summer. It was blisteringly hot and dry.

Then, on August 9, the Manson "Family" murdered Sharon Tate, Abigail Folger, Jay Sebring, Voytek Frykowski, and Steven Parent in a Benedict Canyon mansion. The next night, Rosemary and Leno LaBianca were killed in their Los Feliz home. A media frenzy ensued. While early conspiracy theories blamed the violence on organized crime, then later on a drug ring, it became increasingly evident that these crimes were committed by a cult-like group led by a charismatic leader who looked and talked like a hippie.

What captured my attention was the fact that the murders had been committed primarily by women. Images of the Manson "girls" were plastered on every TV broadcast and newspaper front-page for months during the 1970 trial. All but one was sentenced to life in prison. Linda Kasabian, nine months pregnant at the time of the Sharon Tate murders, had traded family secrets for her freedom.

I remember being transfixed by the Manson girls—their dirty peasant dresses hanging off their wiry frames, the Xs carved into their foreheads, the vacant expressions of their mug shots, their disruptive presence during the trial. I knew I was supposed to find them repellent, but I secretly enjoyed imagining their lives—taking drugs and having sex on a ranch in the middle of the desert or at a celebrity home in Topanga Canyon, practically in my own backyard. I was especially fascinated by Linda Kasabian, the one who saved her own life.

The Manson girls were the first public figures to make an impression on me, to make me think about the world outside suburbia. They made me realize that girls could reject the values they were raised with, that some girls went over the edge of acceptable behavior. My attraction to them was confusing, a little embarrassing. I didn't talk about it. It felt related in some way to the other secret I kept—the one about those queer feelings I had but didn't know how to articulate, or with whom to identify.

As I got older, I started to read books about that era—Vincent Bugliosi's paranoid *Helter Skelter*, Ed Sanders' insider-y *The Family*, Joan Didion's evocative *The White Album*. I would look for details about the girls or their lives, hoping to make sense of my fascination. But often, when I'd scratch the surface I'd only find more surface.

Public figures easily become symbols, ideas, icons. But the fascination doesn't diminish. What I've come to realize is that in looking for them, I look for myself as well. As I deepen my knowledge of the women of that era, I deepen my understanding of this formative time in my life.

Suddenly no one in the suburbs felt safe anymore, especially in Los Angeles. My mother and I continued to sit by the pool every day, but her pleasure that summer was mitigated by fear. Perhaps she was uneasy, gripped with anxiety about the changes that were occurring in and around our lives. I absorbed the sense that nothing could protect us, but I was also drawn to the world that was dangerous and swirling out of control.

"We tell ourselves stories in order to live," wrote Joan Didion at the beginning of *The White Album*, in which, among many stories, Didion tells hers about getting to know Linda Kasabian. For Didion, the late 1960s was a time when the imposition of a narrative line that could once make sense of the world started to fall apart. All her expectations for order had imploded. It was a time when violence entered people's lives in the form of the Manson murders, the Vietnam War, assassinations, and politically motivated bombings in major cities on a weekly basis. "I began to doubt the premises of all the stories I had ever told myself," Didion wrote.

Having grown up in the 1970s, I never expect things to line up in a narrative that makes sense of the world. Nonetheless I search for meaning, and often I construct that meaning through the stories of other people. I frame my own story by the icons who have pervaded my consciousness at crucial times in my life. There's some affinity, challenge, desire that underlies my fascination. It's not always clear to me why I'm drawn to particular public figures, but I'm learning to find pleasure in that uncertainty.

A few years ago I spent an evening with Elizabeth Wurtzel, who is perhaps best known for writing books and essays about herself. It was my first time meeting her, and I was hoping to talk about working together on something for the Feminist Press. I have not seen or spoken with her since, but a conversation we had that evening stayed with me. Elizabeth told me a story about a book she never wrote.

A corporate publisher was planning a series of short biographies by famous writers, and they asked her to propose a subject. She wanted to write about Amy Winehouse.

Apparently the publisher was not interested. Elizabeth didn't say exactly why they turned her down, but just that it wasn't going to happen because Amy Winehouse was not the kind of subject they had in mind.

I was immediately drawn to this idea. Not only because I couldn't stop thinking about Amy Winehouse, who had died just a short time before this meeting. But also because I sensed that Elizabeth would tell her own story in a different way by writing about Amy Winehouse, and I wanted to know Elizabeth better. I told her that I would love to publish such a work. She shrugged and changed the subject. A bit later, I circled back to the topic, and she agreed, it would have been a great project. She already had a title: "You Know I'm No Good."

We had planned to meet at a restaurant but instead had met at a Mercer Street loft she was renting. We drank wine as we talked and listened to records. After awhile, she seemed more interested in the music than the conversation, so I suggested we listen to Winehouse's *Back to Black*.

I don't have it, she said.

She only had the one song, "You Know I'm No Good." That's the only music by Amy Winehouse she was listening to. That's apparently all she needed to know.

I began to imagine how other writers might respond, given the chance to write about their icons, and asked some of my favorites to contribute to this book. The answers were totally unpredictable. I am stunned by the emotional intensity they have each brought to this project. I've always thought that the weirdest thing about celebrity culture is the level of intimacy we feel with people we don't know. These contributors explore the depths of such haunted relationships with disarming grace, and in the process, reveal themselves.

MARY GAITSKILL

on

LINDA LOVELACE

Icon of freedom, innocent carnality; icon of brokenness, and confusion; icon of a wound turned into or disguised as pleasure-source; icon of sexual victimization, sexual power, irreconcilable oppositions; icon of 1970s America; icon of Everywoman. And just another skinny white girl with average looks and a little flat voice, a type you barely notice even if some version of her is everywhere.

I saw Linda Lovelace* in *Deep Throat* because my boyfriend was the projectionist at a hippie film co-op. It was 1972 and I was seventeen. My boyfriend was twenty-five and neither of us was interested in porn which we thought of as a corny old-person thing. But *Deep Throat*, an X-rated comedy about a woman whose clitoris is in her throat, was supposed to be something different, and we were curious, then won over by the film's dirty goofballery. "She just seemed to like it so much," said my boyfriend, and his voice was not salacious as much as tickled. I liked it too, it was funny—but *liking* and arousal are very different. I wasn't excited by *Deep Throat*, and the only thing I could really remember about it afterward

---

*Linda Borman was the given name of the porn actress known as Linda Lovelace. I am choosing to use the adopted name "Lovelace" because that apparently contradictory persona is who and what I am writing about here.

was Lovelace's sweet smile and the strange expression in her eyes, a look that I could not define and still can't, a look that was not happy yet that seemed to go with her smile.

I was however wildly excited by the next movie I saw at the co-op, a film that on the face of it has nothing in common with *Deep Throat*, but which remains, in my imagination, weirdly linked with the porn comedy; it was Carl Dreyer's *The Passion of Joan of Arc*, an emotionally stunning silent film made in 1928 about the persecution, psychological torture, and death of an inexplicably, helplessly powerful nineteen-year-old girl. I'm sure it sounds ridiculously arty, but trust me, my reaction was not artistic. I was horrified by this film, but also moved and so aroused that I was embarrassed to be in public, even in the dark. I don't *like* images of persecution or death or torture, but liking was irrelevant; *Passion* demanded a powerful response and my body gave it.

Anyway, in 1980, when Linda Lovelace wrote a book (with journalist Mike McGrady) about her experience called *Ordeal*, then joined Catharine MacKinnon's antiporn movement, I fleetingly remembered her sweet, strange-eyed smile, and how different it seemed from the woman claiming that anyone who watched *Deep Throat* was watching her being raped. I was vaguely sad but not that surprised; it seemed just one more piece of senseless effluvia flying past.

Fast-forward to 2012, when not one but two mainstream biopics about Linda Lovelace were being made at the same time, I learned of these films because of a brief involvement with a guy who had some vague connection with one of the films as well as very strong opinions on its subject. He felt nothing but contempt for Lovelace, whom he described as a deeply stupid liar who refused to take responsibility for any of her actions, including her participation in pre-*Throat* porn loops, particularly one in which she enthusiastically received a dog. He told me that in *Ordeal* she claimed, among other things, that she was forced by her husband/pimp, Chuck Traynor, to "do" the dog, but that "everyone" knew it was a lie, that she was "into it," that is, she liked it.

This was all news to me, but I shrugged and said, I don't blame her. We've all done things that, while not embarrassing in our own private self-scape, *would* be embarrassing if projected on a public movie screen. Besides she had kids. If you had kids, would you want to talk about dog-fucking with them? My friend said she turned on Women Against Pornography and said *they* used her too. I said, they probably did; those women are bonkers. He came back, but *then* she posed for a magazine called *Leg Show*, to which I said, so what, that's not really porn and she probably needed the money. We changed the subject and broke up later that night.

But the conversation made me care about Linda Lovelace in a way I previously had not, and made me want to defend her. It also made me curious. Lovelace and her husband/pimp Chuck Traynor are dead (both in 2002), as is *Deep Throat* director Gerry Damiano and Lovelace's costar Harry Reems, so why was a grown man talking like a school-yard bully about her ten years later? Why was her story suddenly of such pop-cultural interest that forty-plus years after *Deep Throat*, two mainstream film companies wanted to tell it?

When the biopic titled *Lovelace* came out the following year (the other, *Inferno*, floundered and was killed), I saw it and became something more than curious. *Lovelace* is a candy-colored, feel-good story of a nice girl forced into porn by an abusive husband, who nonetheless blooms with the attention of celebrities like Hugh Hefner, is redeemed by feminism, is accepted by her family, gets married, and starts a family of her own. Critics and viewers responded tepidly, but to me the bowdlerization was even more obnoxious than my former friend's contempt. Why, after more than forty years, were people so insistently sanitizing and simplifying this story?

I suppose I shouldn't have wondered. *Deep Throat* was an extreme phenomenon that, whimsically and unselfconsciously, confirmed and challenged the status quo of masculine privilege by creating a fantasy world of blowjobs that gave pride of place to female orgasm. This preposterous polarity was heightened by the film's combination of high and low (in terms of register or pitch), the way it put together silliness and lightness of spirit with the florid id-imagery of porn, especially the image of its star, an appealing girl happily splitting her pretty face to get hairy dick impossibly far down her throat. Made in six days for $45,500, with sitcom dialogue and a kooky soundtrack, the film grossed $50 million: *Screw*'s Al Goldstein fell in love, the mafia made a killing (literally), President Nixon condemned it, New York

Mayor Lindsay banned it, and the glitterati lined up to see it, including Jack Nicholson, Truman Capote, Liz Taylor, and Jackie O. Harry Reems was arrested and eventually did time for obscenity; Linda Lovelace became an international celebrity.

She may've been average-looking, but (in addition to her famous erotic "trick" and her ardent way with it) Lovelace projected the perverse charm of innocence soiled but blithely so, a fragile, playful persona that was uniquely, darkly radiant, dirty and ethereal both. She appeared at a time that is hard to imagine now, when porn has become normalized and commodified to the point that middle-class teenagers might sport license plates that read PORN STAR and actual porn stars are featured in mainstream news websites. Nineteen seventy-two was a transitional time, both libertine and innocent in every direction, with traditional values asserted as aggressively as they were rebelled against. It was a time when many people must've found it wonderful to see a sweet-faced young woman with a touchingly delicate figure and a girly voice swallowing throbbin' gristle till her nose ran, yet whom you could watch without feeling nasty *because she liked it so much.* The 2005 documentary *Inside Deep Throat* includes footage of a press conference at which Lovelace appears in a long, pale gown with a rose in her teeth; she looks anything but average. She is beautiful, puckishly so, and surrounded by absolutely gaga men who look as if they are witnessing the arrival of a woman riding in from another world astride a thunderbolt, a world in which good and evil bang together (pun intended) with joy, and *anything* is allowed without consequence.

It is poignant to consider this explosion of glamour and sexual exuberance emanating from an utterly unglamorous, abused and abusing couple, but—for a minute it seemed like anything was allowed, and when anything is allowed, what really *is* abuse?

Abused or not, Lovelace suddenly had offers she never dreamed of, from television, movies, and lecture circuits, and she gamely tried to make use of it all, trollish husband in tow. But either because she lacked the talent or because she was simply too overwhelmed by the whole thing, none of it worked for her. She dropped out of sight, divorcing Chuck and marrying childhood friend Larry Marchiano. Until that is, she produced *Ordeal* and re-emerged as an antiporn activist. Her besotted fans were disappointed; her former colleagues were *angry*, and in some cases hurt—according to porn star Annie Sprinkle, *Deep Throat's* director was "heartbroken" by her claims.

The Other Hollywood, by Legs McNeil and Jennifer Osborne (with Peter Pavia), is an "Uncensored Oral History of the Porn Film Industry," and it is jammed with people expressing their anger and disgust at Lovelace—even people who plainly state that yes, Chuck Traynor beat his wife. "I mean, this was a woman who never took responsibility for her own shitty choices—but instead blamed everything that happened in her life on porn. You know, 'The devil made me do it.'" (Gloria Leonard, 267) In a personal exchange with me, Annie Sprinkle was gentler about it: "I do think Linda was in an abusive relationship. And she was definitely traumatized by it . . . And I strongly believe that she had a ball doing *Deep Throat* and that she was treated like a star, and went through a horrible time simultaneously with her husband . . . I'm sure she also associated *Deep Throat* with that horrible time in her life."

I liked that interpretation and took it further, possibly in a too-romantic direction. I thought that the relationship must've at least started as consensual, that there was probably an element of coercion from Chuck, that what she was feeling then was part fear and part willing excitement, but at some point the excitement tipped over into real fear, and eventually Lovelace could not tell where one ended and the other began. I wondered if Traynor, pimp that he was, knew for sure. Once out of the relationship, I imagined that Lovelace simply lacked the confidence to describe what she did and felt in a nuanced way, and that it was very, very nuanced and contradictory. So she went with either "I liked it" or "I was raped."

This is a very rational, mild, and forgiving way to think of an experience that was none of the above. Just how "none of the above" it might've been became apparent when I read *Ordeal*. That book, which is now out of print, has been so dismissed that I almost didn't read it. I can see why it was dismissed; the experience it describes is so relentlessly, ridiculously miserable, so helpless and hapless, so utterly incongruous with how Lovelace initially presented herself. Some of it does strain credulity; as I read the beginning of it, I asked myself out loud, "Where were her instincts?" It's a good question: if her portrayal of Chuck Traynor is at all accurate, he was the kind of guy that even a very young and naïve girl could see coming from a mile off; you don't need special shrewdness or even much experience to recognize a predator, all you need is animal instinct. But some people's instincts have been ruined. Some people's instincts have been so ruined by such disrespectful treatment that, for them, disrespect is not merely a norm, it has a kind of hyper-reality. Such people don't necessarily identify as masochistic in a conscious way. They are sometimes just weird people whose strange ways of dealing with the world can make them a pain in the ass. It's hard to want to know them, that is, to know how hurt they are, and how intractable the damage is. I don't quite believe everything in *Ordeal*, but even if half of it is true, the "horrible time in her life" was neither nuanced nor contradictory, and at no point involved "having a ball" or "being treated like a star."

But, while it expresses a low opinion of porn, *Ordeal* doesn't actually blame porn for anything. The book is appreciative of some people in the business (for example the late porn star Andrea True) and depicts *Deep Throat* as a big step up from the stuff Lovelace says she was forced into previously. She describes Gerry Damiano and most of the other people involved with the film as relatively decent and considerate, including a soundman who offered to protect her from Traynor if she gave him a "signal." As grotesque as it is, I can't dismiss it; too much of it rings true. But it's also impossible to dismiss the appealing, even delightful way she looks in *Deep Throat*, or her otherworldly radiance in the following press conferences and interviews. In spite of her eerie, sometimes dead-looking eyes, there is nothing in her voice or body language that suggests terror or victimization, not even during a scene in which she's pretending to be menaced by a pretend rapist with a gun. Really, she *does* look like she's having a ball. A ball in hell maybe, but a ball nonetheless.

This equal-and-opposite mixed signage is what makes Lovelace a compelling, even profound figure, a lost soul and powerful icon, defiled innocent, sexual rock star who posed for a skin mag at fifty-two. All these years later, her redemption is important for feminists (and not only those with an antiporn fixation) because, in spite of her Sadeian trajectory, her experience is a fun-house version of the sometimes excruciating contradictions that many women experience in relation to sex.

Consider this mild and typical anecdote: a friend of mine, now in her fifties, told me how, in her twenties, she used to walk into the St. Mark's Bar and Grill and every time she did, this same guy would grab her breasts and everybody would laugh. She said thinking about it now made her furious. When I asked her what she did at the time, she said she laughed too because she didn't know what else to do. And I remember what she was like in her twenties; she flirted and giggled a lot, and loved attention. So which is true, the giggly girl who just laughed when the guy grabbed her, or the angry woman in her fifties? Now consider this more extreme contradiction: a therapist once told me that some women orgasm when they are raped. I had never heard this before and found it hard to believe. I said, "So, if the rapist said 'she liked it,' he would be telling the truth." The therapist said, no, she did not like it. But for some people the adrenal arousal of terror turns into global arousal that becomes sexual.

I thought of that when I read in *The Other Hollywood* that Linda was constantly turned on, that she was "soaking wet," and that she really seemed to be "into it" with the dog. In *Ordeal*, Lovelace writes that she was forced into the scene with the dog, that there was actually a gun on the set. But in *The Other Hollywood*, actress Sharon Mitchell says that when she briefly walked onto the set it "didn't look like they were forcing her to do anything," rather that it "looked like they were forcing the dogs!" Mitchell says that she was so upset by the sight of Linda's arousal that she became terrified and ran down the stairs (51). The first striking thing about this anecdote is Mitchell's mean-girl brutality; she didn't realize how many people would say the same shit about her? Was the sight of arousal really so terrifying? Or was she running from terror itself, terror wound together with arousal so tight that she didn't consciously know what she was looking at or running from? The second striking thing is that although everyone else involved describes one dog on the set, Mitchell apparently saw "dogs"—kind of like Lovelace seeing a gun that everyone else says wasn't there. Chuck Traynor did hit Linda and he did own guns. If he ever pointed a gun at Linda, even once, in her mind it was probably always there.

Or not. Maybe there was no gun and she knew it. Maybe she was terrified anyway. Fear is powerful sometimes even when there is no immediate threat. Sometimes it motivates people without their knowing it except in hindsight, if at all.

When I was seventeen I was violently raped. It was horrible, but I got through it and did not believe it affected me overmuch. It did not inhibit me sexually; in the years following the experience I was promiscuous, even aggressively so. Sometimes I had sex without really knowing why, but that seemed true of many, many people at the time. Then one day when I was nineteen something happened. I was with a guy and we were fooling around on my bed, still fully clothed. Playfully, he raised himself over me, grabbed my wrists, and pinned them. I went completely blank. I don't know how else to describe it. As he put it later, my body went limp and my eyes "empty." Scared himself, he let go of me and said something like "What's wrong?" I said, "I thought you were going to start hitting me." Shocked and upset he replied, "I would never do that, how could you think that?" I said "I don't know," and I meant it. I had no idea how much fear I'd been carrying and was so surprised by my own blanking out that I didn't even understand it at first. We talked some—I don't remember if I told him about being raped or not—but sex was out of the question.

That incident made me realize that I was sometimes having sex because I was afraid that if I didn't I would be raped, even when the men in question did not threaten me in any way. This was definitely not always the case, I had natural feelings. But sometimes fear motivated me without my being aware of it until that one boy's gesture brought it out of hiding. Even then it was so *physically* present in me that I couldn't stop having sex I didn't fully want for almost two years after I realized what was going on.

Because of experiences like this—not just mine, but those that other women have described to me—it's hard for me to see the Lovelace story as a simple matter of lying or not. Even if there was no gun and Lovelace knew it and lied—I can't see that kind of lie as coming from one simple motivation. Maybe Lovelace enjoyed what she did to the point of wallowing in it, including the abuse that came with it, and then years later, when she was ravaged, angry, and broke, rewrote it and came to believe the revision. Maybe she started out liking it and came to hate it, or liked it sometimes and hated it other times. Maybe she never *liked* it, but was masochistically *aroused* by it, or maybe she hated it straight-up but did it anyway. Not many people could describe experiencing any of this accurately let alone honestly, especially if it was *all* true, that is, if she felt all of the above in some hellish combination, and was so torn by the opposition that she developed a fragmented public self, one which smiled and was delightful when prompted, or which assumed an antiporn stance when prompted, with nothing fully developed in support of either.

This last, terrible idea makes me remember my stunned blankness of so long ago, blankness that I acted out of for years and that, frankly, was not about a single act of rape. Blankness is a kind of dead zone, and action that comes from blankness happens in fragments. I know what it's like to be pulled in too many directions to make sense of, but to want to live and to engage so much that you act regardless. It's a hard way to be, but at least I had the space and time to try and understand my experience as best I could. Lovelace didn't have that ordinary luxury because of her fame. Being famous for being yourself is now an American fixation; Linda Lovelace lived the dream, and how. But what would it be like to be famous for being yourself if you didn't know what your "self" was? Imagine projecting and being projected into the world, on a massive scale, as someone who has no complex emotions, who is all persona, in this case a persona that is all about having one particular kind of sex with whomever. Because people liked the persona, it must've felt good at first, hell, it must've felt *great*. Some of the worst things in the world feel that way. At first.

In the documentary *The Real Linda Lovelace* Chuck Traynor described his wife this way: "Everything she did, she had to be told how to do it and when to do it and why she was doing it . . . you always had to tell her what to do." It's self-serving; it's possibly true. After Traynor and Lovelace split, he married Marilyn Chambers, and by most accounts the relationship was good for the eleven years that it lasted. Eric Danville, a friend and fan of Lovelace (and author of *The Complete Linda Lovelace*), once asked Chambers if she ever met Linda. She said no, but that she once overheard her screaming at Chuck on the phone while he winced and held the receiver away from his ear. In an interview she gave before her death in 2009, Chambers was asked what it was like to be married to "the infamous Chuck Traynor" and she defended him all the way, characterizing Lovelace's book as "75 percent BS" and Chuck as "an average Joe Blow kind of guy" who knew what "turned on the average guy."* According to a 2013 article by Christine Pelisek in *The Daily Beast*, Chambers acknowledged that Traynor did hit her once but that she "hit him back really hard," breaking two fingernails; she said that Linda's problem was that she was "meek." The same *Beast* article reports that when Chambers and Traynor divorced, she gave him all of her money, that she died with nothing. That Chambers accepted the rules of the pimp's game, and played by it till the very end, even to her disadvantage, suggests a kind of gallantry or integrity that I admire. But I don't understand why she needed to disparage Lovelace for being "meek" or (it seems to me) for not really knowing that she was actually playing a game let alone what the rules were.

That I saw *The Passion of Joan of Arc* in such close proximity to *Deep Throat* is strictly random. Still I am haunted by it. Lovelace was apparently as hapless as St. Joan was fanatically determined, seemingly as ordinary as St. Joan was extraor-

*See girlsandcorpses.com.

dinary. Yet, like Joan of Arc embodied social and spiritual forces that were most likely beyond her personality, Lovelace was fated to embody extreme and opposing social and sexual forces much too big for the limits of her self, for any self. Both women were torn apart by that which they embodied, yet for a moment glowed with enormous symbolic power. This is what seems the most painful thing about the Lovelace story, more painful even than domestic abuse, to live as a public vector for oppositions that are still too much for this culture, possibly any culture to countenance, to burn with the strength of those forces without fully being able to understand or effectively wield them.

In the end Lovelace divorced Marchiano, claiming that he too abused her. She was poor and sick with hepatitis, and, having fallen out with the antiporn movement, was appearing at porn memorabilia conventions to sign DVD copies of *Deep Throat* and *Ordeal*. The recent film doesn't touch any of this, perhaps because the filmmakers felt that in omitting these aspects of the story they were casting their subject in a positive, more sympathetic light, making it easier for the audience to like her. But the bowdlerization does Lovelace a great disservice. As much as anything, her story is about enormous loneliness and the struggle to survive, a condition so much bigger than how she was seen, through the lens of feminism or porn, and which defies a happy ending.

During *Passion*, one of the twisted inquisitors asks Joan if St. Michael actually spoke to her. As the critic Roger Ebert described it, her face "seems to suggest that whatever happened between Michael and herself was so beyond the scope of the question that no answer is conceivable." The question of whether or not Linda Lovelace was a liar or a victim might be a joke in comparison—but still, I think that whatever happened in that place and time in her life is far beyond the scope of the question.

MARY GAITSKILL is the author of two novels (most recently *Veronica*) and three books of stories (most recently *Don't Cry*). Her essays and stories have been widely anthologized.

JOHANNA FATEMAN

on

ANDREA DWORKIN

JULY

In the nearly empty playground, I watched my daughter push a pretend baby in a swing. It was hot and overcast, and I thought about an email I had received from Amy the day before. She had proposed that I choose an icon to write about, someone who fascinates me. But nobody had come to mind. Not really, not immediately. Not the way I felt an icon should.

An icon is a religious painting, right? I pictured cracking tempera and gold leaf behind glass at the Met, Jesus as a tiny adult in the arms of a giant Mary. My kid twisted the swing's chains and it rose until she could barely reach the bottom of the seat. Then, hanging on, she lifted her feet off the ground so the chains unraveled, spinning her. She let go, or lost her grip, and she smacked the rubbery ground pretty hard before staggering up to do it again. It looked fun, and there was no one around to judge me for allowing it. Her palms and her knees and her striped T-shirt darkened with New York City playground soot. So what?

Inspiration can be terrifying, but when it appears, you have to stare right at it, imagine your life under its sign. If it slams all the doors shut and chases you down a narrow corridor, if it rewrites your life in a matter of minutes, revealing everything that came before as an exercise to prepare you for its unique and superior challenges—well, then, that's the feeling I wanted. As the chains clanked and the birds chirped, I gazed across the park into the trees, running through icons. I became systematic.

I eliminated men, the living, the fashionable, anyone who had not been slandered and spat upon, anyone wishy-washy or too well loved, anyone who had not truly moved me, and anyone who anybody might predict that I'd choose.

I looked at my phone. I let it fall to the bottom of my bag. And then gradually I felt a rich dread coming on, something that might really sustain me. At first I saw her name in type, then I saw it in my handwriting. Then I saw her. Andrea Dworkin, frozen in time at the helm of a failed crusade, reviled and discredited by woman-haters and my feminist peers alike. Andrea Dworkin, the quintessential antipornography feminist, I thought, is totally iconic. I texted Lisa.

With a bad landing, the game with the swing was over, and I hugged my sweaty, tearful three-year-old on the hot park bench. I told myself I wasn't choosing Dworkin to be contrarian or perverse—those weren't the only reasons. And I swore I would never exploit a caricature. But the thing is, caricature cuts both ways. What opens one to ridicule may also make you an icon, and fat, fuck-you Andrea Dworkin was in me like a flame. I saw her recklessly unkempt, noncompliant. I saw her at a podium, or with a picket sign, out there, wherever, always, always in overalls.

A spot on my back burned from a metal bolt in the bench. Now, long after sudden inspiration has settled into committed obsession, after I've read, very carefully, every book by Andrea Dworkin, and spent many days, countless hours, at that same playground thinking about her, I'll admit I can't recall every detail from that day at the park in July 2012. But I do remember this feeling: an adrenaline certainty, that fleeting pleasure just before an idea gets pulled down by the difficulties of actualizing it and the pain of what you think other people will think.

On the bench that day I savored my image of Dworkin, the rebuke of her person, the aesthetic rigor of the overalls. Hugging my sighing, dirty kid, and looking down at the hem of my stupid red sundress and the tops of my female ankle socks, I thought, I get it: Face this stupid question—what to wear—once and for all. Turn your body into a block, a denim plane.

The overalls, common to the countercultural milieu from which Dworkin emerged in revolt in the early 70s, were a uniform not because an army of women wore them, but because she wore them every day. Through repetition, she transformed them from a vague hippie salute to the proletariat to a symbol of personal militancy that was left of the Left, and then off the map. As a formal strategy and a practical solution, they were a stroke of genius.

Would I interview people, I wondered? Would I find out exactly when she adopted the overalls? Did the overalls-as-uniform thing evolve over time, or was it an impulsive vow? I imagined the buckles at her collarbone heating like the bolts in the bench and the chains of the swing. I pictured them rendered in gold and fastened to a blue tempera breastplate. Painted in this manner, an armored saint is an icon. Not that Andrea Dworkin was a saint.

Soon, I would struggle to recast my subject as a choice arrived at logically, and I'd pretend that I had considered a number of historical figures. For weeks, I would act as if I were unsure. "I'm still thinking about it," I'd say. But as we left the park, holding hands and laughing, I was giddy with the sense of my project's inevitability.

I don't know what my daughter was laughing at as we walked down the hill, maybe a dog, but I was laughing in a sort of complicated way at how uncool it is to hate pornography, at how Dworkin's been uncool for so long. I was laughing not because anything was actually funny, but because I was pleased and stunned that a timer had gone off somewhere—in me, obviously, but maybe outside me too, in culture. I thought it was time to go get the baby out of the bathwater. And I was confident; I thought I was just the one to do it.

When we got home I dragged a chair over to the high shelf to get my old diaries down. It was hard to believe how many there were, and it took a long time to find the right ones, but I knew they were from the square, spiral-bound sketchbook phase. Eventually, with an armful laid out on the bed, I determined that it was for a little over a year, twenty years ago, that I was into Dworkin. I blushed, flipping through the teenage record of boiling blood, looking for her name, for my Dworkin period. It started the summer after my first year of college. I was alone mostly, reading in the attic of a house in Portland, Oregon. My bed was by the window and I looked out at the wall of a cemetery.

At eighteen, you're pretty close to thirteen, that age when new surveillance comes with the warm weather, when the words spoken from a car slowing down beside you and the secrets your friends keep are bullet points beneath a subject heading you can't quite make out. Your brain stretches past your boobs but also feels limited by them. By eighteen, there's no denying it: insults have accumulated, the double standard has doubled, and you find out there's a real thing called "feminism" which is, if not a current political movement, at least a number of books. Maybe you've felt that you were drifting at times, but now it's obvious you were moving toward something, you were caught in the pull of a recent philosophical tradition. Now that you can name it, you can find more of it, do lines of it. Dunk your whole head in 'til you can't stand it anymore.

I wanted to be an artist. So it was logical to study female mastery and alienation. How could Dworkin shift so quickly between cold exposition and lyric invective, or between bravado and abjection? How is it possible for writing to have a geological quality and also to not give a fuck? I wanted to know. But I wasn't concerned purely with the formal aspects of her work, or interested in something like "the performance of rage." For me, the political argument was important. Her awful clarity was seductive to a girl in search of a principled revolt. I liked the idea of facing men down, of passing the ERA. I wanted to become an abortionist, break windows, and pour blood on a stack of Penthouse magazines.

After I texted back and forth a few times with Lisa, I told Greg. He got it too. He understood why it was both smart and cool to write about Andrea Dworkin. In fact, he had a copy of her book *Right-Wing Women* in his apartment around the corner and he brought it to me. I was still high: I told him that I already had the title. (The underground filmmaker Jack Smith once stated that the title is 50 percent of an artwork, so I was already halfway done!) I said, "I think I'll call my book *Amerikan Woman.* You know, with a 'K,' the way she spelled it." Greg liked the title. He knew why it was funny for me to choose it. The 1970 hit "American Woman" by the Canadian band The Guess Who gets stuck in my head all the time—sometimes the main guitar riff, or that lead guitar part, but more often I sing, over and over again, the lines, "American woman, stay away from me/American woman, mama, let me be."

Maybe all these years, as I have put on eyeliner, rifled through my desk looking for stamps, sipped club soda on airplanes, and wiped crumbs from the counter into my palm, absently singing the hook of this hard rock masterpiece, I have been unconsciously singing it with a "K." Maybe, using Dworkin's preferred spelling, I've secretly been singing it about her. Or *to* her: "Amerikan woman, stay away from me/Amerikan woman, mama, let me be." She would get the joke.

"Colored lights can hypnotize/Sparkle someone else's eyes/ Now woman, I said get away . . ."

She'd understand the absurdity of the long-haired Canadian singer's plaintive misogyny. His ridiculousness. As the song progresses, he gets to the point. In his political critique, a female temptress—a demanding groupie?—represents the horror of Amerika: "I don't need your war machines/I don't I need your ghetto scenes . . ."

The song was recorded in August of 1969, days after Charles Manson hoped to ignite a race war through the brutal Tate and LaBianca murders. It was released the following January. In the intervening months, Fred Hampton, a rising leader of the Black Panther Party, was assassinated in his sleep by Chicago cops during a raid, and details of the My Lai Massacre—the rapes and mutilations, the slaughter of at least 347 Vietnamese civilians by US soldiers—became public. The day after the song reached the number one spot on the US Billboard Hot 100, in May of 1970, four unarmed students were slain by the Ohio National Guard at Kent State University during an antiwar protest staged in response to Nixon's announcement of The Cambodian Campaign.

Who did The Guess Who think of when they played that song? Which Amerikan woman? I imagine a moon-faced Manson girl through the screen door on Cielo Drive, Hampton's pregnant girlfriend, who slept beside him on the mattress that night, fourteen-year-old Mary Ann Vecchio kneeling by Jeff Miller's dead body at Kent State in that famous photo, and, of course, I see Andrea Dworkin, even though she was unknown and basically invisible during this particular, terrible stretch of US history.

The song peaked at number 4 in 1970 in the Netherlands, where Dworkin, an Amerikan expatriate originally from Camden, New Jersey, a recent graduate from Bennington College, was being tied up, punched, kicked, and burned with cigarettes by a fellow radical. A girlhood at war with hypocrisy had prepared her for her teen years against the war (seething poetry and shit work for the cause), but nothing had prepared her for her first marriage. The burn wounds on her breasts wouldn't ever fully heal, they continued to periodically, spontaneously open and bleed like stigmata.

Elsewhere, the women's movement was happening. It was even selling books. Shulamith Firestone's *The Dialectic of Sex* appeared in 1970, introducing the radical feminist concept of the sex class system and calling for the destruction of the nuclear family. Kate Millett's brilliant text *Sexual Politics*, published the year before, would light the path for Dworkin's own literary criticism, the passionate and idiosyncratic methodology at the heart of her finest philosophical writing. But Dworkin hadn't read it by her twenty-fifth birthday in 1971. She was still trapped in an apartment, married, "nearly dead, almost catatonic," she'd later write. By the time she turned twenty-six she had escaped. Destitute, living as a fugitive (he stalked her), she was, in her words, "an infant born out of a corpse, still with the smell of death on her, but hating death." And she was writing a book.

I love the song "Amerikan Woman." Though I like the Lenny Kravitz cover from 1999 also, my favorite version is the original; my favorite video is the first one that comes up first when you search for "the guess who 1970"; and my favorite comment on that video is this one:

> What i cant believe is that all you cunts are arguing politics and no one ever mentioned that Randy Bachmann is playing one of the most recognizable leads in guitar history and this numbskull camera man is focused on the bloody fucking bass player.

It puts things in perspective.

I used to be in a feminist punk band, now I own a hair salon and pretend to be an art critic. Sometimes, I agree to be shut in a small recording studio in a corporate office to write pop songs with complete strangers as per a folly of a contract that I signed in 2010 that paid the bills in 2011. I'm cheerful about it because, who knows, maybe there's a hit sleeping inside me, but this potential, like everything else in my life, is sharply constrained by the overarching thing that I am: a mother since 2009, fulfilled but restless, happily in a deep malaise, and always tired.

Luckily, I've found one solution to my predicament, one way to feel like myself again, to stand tall at a slight distance from the joy/boredom dialectic that structures my days. I've figured out how to be a rebel while still performing to my own high standard of responsibleness. I've begun to tell people when I run into them on the street or talk to them at parties, when they stop by the salon, or when they ask me in emails what I'm up to, that I'm writing a book—a book, not just an essay—about Andrea Dworkin. And if they ask me why, I make up a reason.

An arrow can't change its course once it's in flight. It's been set in motion, shot high into the air, and that's that. All I can do now is thank myself—or curse myself—for, at some point in my teenage past, closing my eyes, holding Andrea Dworkin in my imperfect heart, and thoughtlessly drawing back the bowstring.

In 1972 she agreed to walk through customs with a briefcase full of heroin in exchange for a plane ticket to New York. When she got here, she had the start of a manuscript. In 1974, the year I was born, her first book *Woman Hating* was published. Part Simone de Beauvoir, part Huey Newton, and something all her own, this urgent, relatively hopeful, radical feminist primer analyzes fairy tales, foot-binding, and witch burning. Dworkin looks at *Story of O* and the porn magazine *Suck*, too. "This book is an action, a political action where revolution is the goal. It has no other purpose," *Woman Hating* begins. And so began Andrea Dworkin's career as a militant and oracular voice of the women's movement.

With revolutionary purpose and aching literary ambition, she wrote more than ten books over three decades, delivering her singular, apocalyptic vision of women's oppression in both nonfiction and novels. *Woman Hating* is an axe, a brilliant start. People love to call *Pornography* a bonfire. *Right-Wing Women* is a razor blade, still applicable, and *Intercourse* is devastatingly canonical. *Mercy*, her last novel, is revolting and transfixing, impossibly simultaneously unhinged and self-aware. Then there are smaller jewels—the speech "The Rape Atrocity and the Boy Next Door," her essays about Jean Rhys and Emily Brontë—but it doesn't matter. The breadth and complexity of her work have been overwritten by her antiporn reputation.

A prophetic orator, she used both the specter of genocide and the pathetic details of ordinary women's terrible lives to support her dire warnings. "In this country in the coming years," she said to the crowd at a lesbian pride rally in 1975, "I think there will be a terrible storm." The rally was held in Central Park, in June, a month after the official end of the Vietnam War. "I think the skies will darken beyond recognition," she predicted. "Those who are raped will see the darkness as they look into the face of the rapist." It's a struggle to picture the audience, hear women clapping for her. Certainly, no one would say something like this at a Pride event today: "Those who are assaulted and brutalized by madmen will stare intently into the darkness to discern who is moving toward them at every moment."

In the late 70s, Dworkin's thundering speeches, delivered at conferences and colleges and rallies and marches, began to focus on pornography. She indicted it as fascist propaganda meant to terrorize women, created to demonstrate their inferiority through the persistent depiction of them as whores hungry for violation and punishment. "Images of women bound, bruised, and maimed on virtually every street corner, on every magazine rack, in every drug store, in movie house after movie house, on billboards, on posters posted on walls, are death threats to a female population in rebellion," she told a small group of students at the University of Massachusetts in the winter of 77. "Female rebellion against male sexual despotism, female rebellion against male sexual authority, is now a reality throughout this country," she continued, assessing the movement's progress. "The men," she accused, "meeting rebellion with an escalation of terror, hang pictures of maimed female bodies in every public place."

Hyperbole, yes. But: the year before, the producer of *Snuff*, a low-budget film about a Manson-like satanic biker gang, courted publicity with the claim that the movie showed the real dismemberment and murder of a woman; and a Sunset Boulevard billboard advertising the Rolling Stones' new album *Black and Blue* showed model Anita Russell in bondage, her legs spread, a dark mark on her inner thigh, and beside her, the text, "I'm 'Black and Blue' from the Rolling Stones—and I love it!"

Dworkin often referred to the ancient Greek origin of the word "pornography." It's literal meaning is not the depiction of nudity or sex acts, but the depiction of pornai, the lowest class of prostitutes, brothel slaves available to all men. She saw pornography as an ancient genre technologized in her day by cynical entrepreneurs of the so-called sexual revolution: the porn industry that emerged in the 70s was rooted in a fraternal antiwar counterculture that had forsaken its female foot soldiers, exploited them—her—for sex, domestic labor, and typing.

The *Antipornography Civil Rights Ordinance* that Dworkin coauthored in 1983 with feminist legal scholar Catharine MacKinnon—a doomed legislative attempt to reframe pornography as a form of sex discrimination—took Dworkin beyond the polarizing sex wars of the women's movement, and put her at the center of a larger public debate. The 1986 Meese Commission's report on pornography included thirty minutes of her brutal, poetic testimony, and she never escaped the tinge of her accidental or strategic alignment with the anti-obscenity Right.

In Dworkin, porn, prostitution, and S/M are inseparable, irredeemable institutions of the sex class system. They exist to keep women inferior. Also, women—as a class, and as a metaphysical category—are victims. For her charismatic inflexibility on these points, she may still be the feminist figure most invoked and refuted in feminist demands for sexual freedom. In our insistence that we have the prerogative to make and use pornography, to choose sex work, to engage in every kind of consensual act, and to do so as revolutionaries, she's the censorial demagogue we shoot down. We can't stand her.

So why do I love her?

That was the question I felt I'd have to answer. And it was much harder to answer in July 2012 than it is now, as I had not yet read—or reread—Dworkin's books. My case for her as an overlooked literary great was built on memory and instinct, a longing for my own immature, politicizing brain.

The next week, back at the hot playground, I stood by the swings again, watching my daughter wind up the chains. I thought hard about what I would tell Amy about my icon. We had a phone date scheduled in a few days. I'd never met her or spoken to her before. We'd only emailed. As far as I knew, all she knew about me was my connection to the riot grrrl movement via the lineage of my ex-band, and that I had donated my papers from the 90s—zines and correspondence mostly—to the Fales Library Riot Grrrl Collection at New York University. Lisa, the archivist at Fales who started the collection, was editing a book of material from the collection. I was going to write an essay for that book as well, and Amy was going to publish it.

I had planned, from the very moment inspiration had come to me, to profit from the element of surprise in choosing Dworkin as my subject, but I didn't look forward to surprising Amy. I cringed, imagining that when I said, "I think I want to write about Andrea Dworkin," she would think that I was proposing a redundant, third-wave critique of a marginal political adversary. I also cringed imagining that she might think I wanted to write a love letter. Yet, wouldn't a love letter be more interesting? You could be both contemporary and critical in one's love letter to a fascist, I thought. Not that Andrea Dworkin was a fascist—but Amy might think so.

In the meantime, I made a plan. I would put my child in preschool and read Dworkin's books in chronological order. I downloaded her complete works from radfem.org and ordered the early titles from used booksellers online. But, I cheated immediately. I went to the Strand and bought *Intercourse*, her seventh book (not including her early chapbooks), which was published simultaneously with her sixth book, the novel *Ice and Fire*, in the United States in 1987. I couldn't resist going out of order and starting with *Intercourse*. I wanted to see if it was as good as I remembered.

I remembered it as mournful and punk, full of "fuck," "fucking," and "the fuck," a long drive, with no stops, in the desert of male genius. And as I sat in Le Pain Quotidien, across the street from the bookstore, drinking hot coffee in air conditioning, trying to conceal the cover as I read, I—again—found her argument lucid, not even extreme, just honest. When you get right down to it, who can deny that the institution of intercourse is the linchpin of heterosexuality, its emblem and climax; that it's an act socially and legally regulated to create and enforce sex difference and thus male supremacy?

Patriarchal metaphysics are rendered voluptuously in *Intercourse*. It's like a Delacroix: wild-eyed horses falling, bayonets, breasts, corpses. Longing, hatred, and history. I love Dworkin's love for the authors she takes apart: Leo

Tolstoy, Kobo Abe, James Baldwin, Tennessee Williams, Isaac Bashevis Singer, and Gustave Flaubert. It's an unsubmissive, un-inferior love. Her arrogant, feminist use of the omniscient voice asserts her expertise, not by exposing herself, but by exploiting her intimate knowledge of these authors. She assembles their testimony about fucking—what it is and means—in a controlled, meticulous argument.

In the edition I had just purchased, there was something new, a preface she wrote in 1995. It's a proper introduction offered in bitter hindsight. She refused to provide one initially, even though her colleagues encouraged her to prepare her readers for the confrontational text, and to protect herself from "bad or malicious readings and purposeful distortions." But, for the occasion of a new edition, after years of such malicious readings, she gave in. This introduction is full of defiant despair at her book's reception: Her achievement was illegible, distorted by her reputation as a man-hating zealot. "*Intercourse* became," she writes, "a Rorschach inkblot in which people saw their fantasy caricatures of me and what they presumed to know about me," she writes. And beyond the toxic antiporn association so particular to her, she points to a broader taboo she's transgressed. Women may vote either yes or no to fucking, she explains. Anything that is not an unequivocal and enthusiastic "yes" is a deadly "no," a woman writer's suicide:

> The range of emotions and ideas expressed by Tolstoy et al. is literally forbidden to contemporary

women. Remorse, sadness, despair, alienation, obsession, fear, greed, hate—all of which men, especially
male artists, express—are simple no votes for women
. . . Critical thought or deep feeling puts one into the
Puritan camp, that hallucinated place of exile where
women with complaints are dumped, after which we
can be abandoned. Why—socially speaking—feed
a woman you can't fuck? Why fuck a woman who
might ask a question let alone have a complex emotional life or a political idea?

Andrea Dworkin was not a light that shut itself off when I
left the room at age twenty or twenty-one, in hot pursuit
of pro-sex feminist thought and postmodernist literature.
She continued to burn with self-reflexive rage; she kept writing. Suddenly, my abandonment of her grieved me terribly.
I thought about how no male artist, however objectionable
philosophically, or in his personal life, prompted the shrink-
ing disavowal I performed when her name came up among
feminists in the subsequent years. Let's say she was half-
wrong. Let's say she was 100 percent wrong wrong wrong.
So what? While I think about the double standard every day,
I don't normally feel like a traitor.

In penance and in fascination I began to take notes. Actually, I copied quotations, whole passages, into a dollar-store
composition book. Too many passages felt exquisitely raw
and blasphemous, like the heart of the matter, a key to the
text, to pass by unremarked, untranscribed. Over the next

few days, I copied a large portion of *Intercourse* by hand. I was angry with myself for doing something so pointless, but I was also defiant: I justified it to myself as a performance, and celebrated my growing sense of futility regarding the project. I told myself I was in the presence of the healthy terror and self-doubt that accompanies anything worth doing.

And when I was not copying *Intercourse*, taking care of my kid, or working, I binged on Dworkin's memoirs and novels. I didn't take any notes at all, because this was leisure.

Also leisure: perusing her website with its aging HTML. Andreadworkin.com was my night-light, an open tab in bed. I felt an uneasy sisterhood with whoever chose the code for the rose, sponge-paint texture of the border, and the digital dark wood panel for the "library" and "memorial" buttons. My visits to this place destroyed any half-conscious hope I had in finding an underdog glamour in Dworkin's critical disrepute. I gave myself over to the heavy sadness inspired by the aesthetics of the abject website and, of course, all of the writing there about rape, battery, and the Holocaust.

The night before I was supposed to talk to Amy, I selected and copied a few lines from one of Dworkin's later speeches and emailed them to myself:

> I suggest to you that if any society took seriously what it means to have half of its population raped, battered as often as women are in both the United States and Canada, we would be turning government

buildings into shelters. We would be opening our churches to women and saying, "You own them. Live in them. Do what you want with them." We would be turning over our universities.

"You own them. Live in them" was the subject line of my email, but until I was on the phone with Amy the next day, I didn't know why that thought, in particular, moved me.

I sat by the window in my apartment and watched people walk through the alley below while Amy and I talked. The basketball court is past the alley, and then there's the gate to the playground. I watched some kids walk up the steps to the gate. I had a notebook open on my lap, but there was not much written on the two pages. On one side there was just a phrase: "the allure of the despised woman." We talked about the icon anthology she was putting together, and about the different writers who would contribute. Eventually, I said nervously, "I'm thinking of writing about Andrea Dworkin." She laughed, surprised, and I said, "I know."

Then I remembered something. A document came up like a wall in front of my thoughts, and though I kept talking, I was thinking of a PDF I downloaded and read on the day I got the first email, the one that suggested I choose someone who fascinates me. That day, before we went to the playground, before I stood by the swings trying to think of an icon, I read, with glum nausea, the "Freeh Report on Pennsylvania State University," the results of the indepen-

dent investigation into the cover-up of the sexual abuse per-
petrated by serial pedophile Gerald A. Sandusky. "The most
saddening finding by the Special Investigative Counsel is the
total and consistent disregard by the most senior leaders at
Penn State for the safety and welfare of Sandusky's child
victims," it read.

I recalled how I followed the news of the scandal as it
unfolded, absorbing the details of Sandusky's crimes, thinking about the institutional protection that Penn State had
afforded him, first as a coach, and then when he ran a char-
ity for underprivileged boys on university property after
his retirement (with an unusual compensation package).
I'd watched the students riot on TV, protesting the action
finally taken by the Board of Trustees, the firing of Coach
Paterno, one of the men who did nothing. The Freeh report,
I guess, was supposed to be the end of this ugly business. I
was transfixed by its officialness, by the evidence assembled,
and by the emails between the men:

> They exhibited a striking lack of empathy for San-
> dusky's victims by failing to inquire as to their safety
> and well-being, especially by not attempting to deter-
> mine the identity of the child who Sandusky assaulted
> in the Lasch building in 2001. Further, they exposed
> this child to additional harm by alerting Sandusky,
> who was the only one who knew the child's identity,
> of what McQueary saw in the shower that night.

I don't know what to do about the villainous compulsion of a Sandusky—do you? The question is how to put blaring sirens of horror and conscience into powerful men whose human reflexes are inhibited, dampened, or absent. Or, is it, more simply, how to strip these men of power?

Take away football forever; shutter the school. Let the protesting students who love sports more than they hate rape stand in a crater where the Lasch building once stood and dig a ditch to hell. That's what I thought. I thought it when I read the PDF on the day I decided to write about Andrea Dworkin, and again while I was on the phone with Amy.

On the notebook page facing the one where I'd written "the allure of the despised women" I had written a few more notes. "The burn book, the diary, the novel. The poem, the speech, the law. The forms explored by the socially suiciding feminist writer."

I don't remember what I said to Amy exactly. The things you do when you're nervous are always a blur. I said something about Penn State, about how it made me crave someone like Dworkin at the height of her powers, a voice advocating the total transformation of society, a voice uninterested in preserving universities. And I'm sure I said some other stuff.

"I like the idea," Amy said, as I watched a police car drive slowly up the alley below my window, and listened closely to her for any clue about how to proceed, what to write. "I like the idea of writing about Andrea, someone who everyone thinks they fundamentally disagree with," she continued, "but then you realize that without her voice, the conversation never goes deep enough. " The conversation about porn, S/M, and sex work, she meant. I told her about Dworkin's out-of-print novels, how they're full of sex. And I told her *Intercourse* is a triumph.

"You'll need to add yourself into the piece," Amy said, I think toward the end of our conversation, "and show where you fit in." She made it sound easy.

I know that the quotation I emailed myself from Dworkin's speech is not a command to turn over Penn State, or the Vatican, or government buildings to the victims. It's not about seizing property to pay reparations. It's simply a speculation, or a suggestion. Also, I know that Sandusky's victims were boys and Dworkin wrote, in that speech, about women. So what?

After the phone call I put glycolic acid all over my face and neck to eat off the dead skin, the top layer of skin, the fine lines. My business partner Shaun turned me on to these acid peels; he figured out we could get the stuff at the wholesale price because we own a hair salon.

When the crawling, burning sensation got too intense I mixed a paste of baking soda and water in my hand and scrubbed the gel off. Looking at my red face in the medicine cabinet mirror, I wondered how one might reconcile the heart of a revolutionary/abortionist with a face and body that capitulate to the demands of looking nice. This is just one small example of the dilemma, if you know what I mean.

I know my generation of feminists is adamant about the radical potential of a bundle of contradictions. And yet, to be completely honest, I'm terribly unsatisfied. Nothing, no one, not a single one of these bitches on the Internet can soothe me with a truism.

AUGUST

At JD's birthday party, at a bar downtown, Becca and I talked about being punk girls in the Northwest in the early 90s. When I first met her, so many years ago, she appeared to be both deep in the Olympia riot grrrl scene and to stand apart from it. I was convinced that she would end up being a real artist, in her real life, later. Also, she never did anything to her hair. Unlike the rest of us, she didn't shave it off, dye it black, bleach it yellow, or cut it into a ragged Louise Brooks bob. She just always had beautiful, long auburn hair. She still does. The party was crowded and we stood, sort of hiding, by a wall, talking about how, at a certain point, things turned bad in our scene. We crossed a line, or some of us did. In an arrogant punk version of what we thought was intersectional feminism, we called everyone a fascist. Self-righteous and guilt-ridden, middle-class white girls distorted the principle of "the personal is political" to buttress petty attacks, and Becca and I felt a little sick thinking back to that time. We congratulated ourselves for not being the worst culprits among our peers. Not by a long shot. I drank a margarita and then another and we agreed that riot grrrl style, intellectual conformity, and fear had poisoned our art. No real action felt possible. It took some time to repair ourselves. Becca said, after a long pause, "It's going to be hard to write about all this shit in your riot grrrl essay for Lisa's book." She was right; it would be hard, especially because by August, I only cared about Andrea Dworkin.

I questioned Becca about Dworkin for a long time. She wouldn't say much, though. She had read part of *Intercourse* in a women's studies class, but it was a haze. She only knew that she rejected it completely from a pro-sex, pro-sex worker standpoint. She seemed to feel bad, in light of my current obsession, to detail her negative impressions of Dworkin, even though I was so hungry for the details. She said she wanted to go back to Dworkin and read her for real.

Matt was there too and we talked about Nazi propaganda. What it feels like to look at it, think about it. He was finishing his film *Teenage*, and part of it is about kids involved with Hitler Youth. Strangely, he'd recently become interested in Dworkin too. He said he was especially curious about her second marriage, to a gay man, John Stoltenberg, who's also a fascinating radical writer. He wanted to know about their relationship. Me too. There was a lot to talk about, and I warned myself not to bring every topic back to Dworkin. As the three of us walked to a restaurant the conversation turned to bedbugs and Matt said he knew about someone who had to have all their books dry cleaned.

Within a few days I discovered that I had bedbugs. I cursed my stacks of newly acquired, used paperbacks: Robin Morgan, Kate Millett, Shulamith Firestone, Catharine MacKinnon, and, of course, tons of Dworkin. I spent all my money on a merciless campaign against the bugs. As a mother, I despaired: three years of organic cotton baby sheets and strawberries only to voluntarily poison the apartment at the first sign of infestation. A guy came with a tank of insecticide. I bagged and unbagged stuff, vacuumed everything, sprayed rubbing alcohol in invisible cracks and every joint of wood. Then I did it again. We stayed outside as much as possible.

Pussy Riot was on trial and JD hurriedly organized an event. She gathered writers and artists to read poems, letters, song lyrics, and court statements by the three members of the Russian art collective who faced charges of "hooliganism motivated by religious hatred" for their guerrilla performance in Moscow's Cathedral of Christ the Savior. JD asked me to be one of the readers. We did it in the basement of the Ace Hotel, on the eve of their verdict and sentencing. That afternoon, before I left for the reading, I untied a garbage bag marked "OK" and pulled out some clothes that had been washed and then dried for at least thirty minutes on high heat. I put a brand new, still-sealed package of bright pink tights into my bag. I walked to Marshall's and bought a seafoam-green dress for seventeen dollars and went to the train. No one could accuse me of carelessly bringing bedbugs to the Pussy Riot event. I felt a little nostalgic doing this familiar thing: going to find JD at a hotel with a costume and a radical text in my purse. On the train downtown I reread one of the sections from the script that I was going to read aloud, Katya's closing statement. Full of mocking insight, pride at their action's success, and without apology, her words made my chest tighten:

> In the end, considering all the irreversible political and symbolic losses caused by our innocent creativity, the authorities decided to protect the public from us and our nonconformist thinking. Thus ended our complicated punk adventure in the Cathedral of Christ the Savior.

I wondered how long her prison sentence would be.

Soon after, I learned of Shulamith Firestone's death, how her body was found in her East Village apartment, a fifth floor walk-up, by the building's owner some days after she passed away. I thought about her retreat from public life after the publication of *The Dialectic of Sex*, about her poverty and mental illness. I looked at the spine of her influential book, tied up in a transparent plastic recycling bag, coated like everything else in my so-called office, with a film of cinnamon oil, some kind of bedbug repellant from Bed Bath & Beyond. I didn't know anymore whether I was keeping bugs in or out. I took Firestone out of the bag to read.

That same day, I received my first google alert for "Andrea Dworkin." I laughed when I saw that she was mentioned in an article by an acquaintance of mine who's a staff writer for a women's lifestyle website. In a personal essay about how she enjoys having her face ejaculated on, my acquaintance uses Dworkin as a symbol of a bygone, prudish feminism that would oppose this sexual practice as degrading. Over the next few months, I'd collect many such mentions of Dworkin.

SEPTEMBER

As the legend goes, nearly a thousand Jews died together at the fortress of Masada. Built by Herod the Great between 37 and 31 BCE on a desolate rock overlooking the Dead Sea, it was a perfect refuge for the brutal and paranoid king. His private palace descended the plateau's northern cliffs in three tiers connected by a rock-cut staircase. A twelve-foot thick wall with thirty-seven defensive towers encircled the barracks, baths, storehouses, synagogue, and administrative buildings of the compound. Ingeniously designed, and protected by forbidding landscape all around, Masada was thought to be unbreachable. And with its stocked storehouses and immense rainwater cisterns, inhabitants could survive there, cut off, indefinitely.

But some seventy years after Herod's death, during the Great Jewish Revolt against the Roman Empire, the Sicarii—a militant sect of Jewish Zealots—seized the fortress in a ruse. They expelled a Roman garrison and lived there for years, conducting raids and harassing imperial authorities until the Roman army began a long siege to crush them.

The Sicarii were trapped, surrounded by orange cliffs, and, at the bottom of the rock, Roman encampments. They watched as the soldiers below constructed an immense ramp against the western face of the rock; they watched them push an iron-plated siege tower and a battering ram up it. But then, when the outer wall was broken and the inner wall was in flames, the Romans retired for the night, leaving their task—the slaughter or enslavement of the Jews—for daylight. In this pause the famous plan was hatched and executed: suicide. The Sicarii would be servants only to God, never the Romans.

"It took a long time," Dworkin writes in her 1990 novel *Mercy*, "it's hard to kill nearly a thousand people one by one, by hand, and they had to hurry because it had to be done before dawn, you can do anything in the dark but dawn comes and it's hard to look at love in the light." The men tenderly slit the throats of their wives and children, laid their bodies in a heap, and burned them. Next, they drew lots to determine which ten men would slay the remainder.

In the PowerPoint presentation I accidentally downloaded, there's an image of ten ancient pottery shards photographed against a black backdrop, each inscribed with a man's name. It's a museum display, I think. These are the men, it suggests, that killed the other men. After they did, one man was selected to slay the remaining nine, which he did, laying their bodies in the blaze before turning his sword against himself. In the morning the Romans, expecting a battle, instead found Masada quiet, the grounds thick with the smoke of burning buildings and a mass cremation.

Mercy is literary endurance art, vomiting and dirge-like, full of rape, cruelty, and destitution. It's not nonfiction, but Dworkin's first-person narrator is called Andrea, and many events and details of the novel coincide with her own biography. The fictional Andrea, like the real Dworkin, is born in 1946, in Camden—a Jewish girl conceived weeks before the liberation of Auschwitz. Andrea and Dworkin are both sexually assaulted in a movie theater at age nine; sexually assaulted in jail after being arrested while protesting the US war in Vietnam. They also have in common a period of prostitution, a love affair on Crete, a need to write, and their spelling of Amerika. They marry Dutch anarchists who torture, injure, and stalk them. They escape Amsterdam for New York in 1972.

We know that in 1974 Dworkin's *Woman Hating* was published, and that she and Stoltenberg fell in love, but in *Mercy*, that doesn't happen. Two brutal years have taken their toll on Andrea. Without money or real friends, she's slept on floors, survived on favors from people she met doing "peace stuff," told people she was a writer, worked on stories all night, shaking with memories of abuse. The retelling of the myth of Masada signals the start of an accelerated phase of her lifelong descent into rage and madness. By 74 she eats from trash cans and lives in a dream. She sets herself on fire outside a porn theater in Times Square. "I go to outside *Deep Throat* where my friend Linda is in the screen," Dworkin writes, "and I put the gasoline on me, I soak myself in it in broad daylight and many go by and no one looks and I am calm, patient, gray on gray cement like the Buddhist monks, and I light the fire; free us."

That's the story's first ending. The final chapter provides an alternate one in which she survives to pick off homeless men. She has sores on her body and her blood is green; she's a soldier in a girl-army of the raped, looking for drunk guys sleeping beneath newspapers or cardboard to attack. The Andrea of *Mercy* is hard to look at. In her, Dworkin merges her feminist arguments with the vengeful fantasies you can't excuse.

My diary from that summer in Portland doesn't say much about *Mercy*, just that I was determined to finish it even though I was tired of reading it, even though I didn't quite know what to make of it. Back then, I couldn't google things in the night. And I didn't have Dworkin's complete works by my bed. But by September of 2012 I did.

I began to cross-reference Dworkin's fiction with her memoirs; and Dworkin's vision of Masada with Josephus's ancient account. I read more recent, more scientific speculations about the fate of the Sicarii. I made a timeline of the modern state of Israel, the archaeological excavation of the Herodian buildings at Masada, and the development of the site as a tourist attraction. I lined it all up with the events of Dworkin's life. This is what I did instead of writing my riot grrrl essay.

I thought about the part in *Mercy* when Andrea recalls a past life as an old woman, as a Zealot on the rock. It's a shameless time-travel device from an author that by 1990, had been so frequently accused of raving she had nothing to lose by embodying the insult, nothing to lose by writing a man-killing character with past lives and her own first name. And it's the occasion for an unpunctuated suicide fantasy—a dense, hallucinatory polemic about Zionism, rape, genocide, and especially about a bloodthirsty, incestuous god—set in a dusty compound overlooking Sodom and Gomorrah almost two thousand years ago.

The old woman hears the men's plan, envisions the orgy of blood waiting, and she declines. She doesn't want to be killed by a man with a blade, doesn't want to be an accessory to his honor, a glorious statement she'd get no credit for. Not a decider, not a killer, a political zero in the middle of nowhere, she won't go down in their defiant show of property destruction, blood pumping from her neck like the smoke pouring from a storehouse. Or perhaps she will go down that way, in history. But she doesn't want to watch the men pin the children down, so she slits her own throat with a sharp rock before the massacre begins.

Toward the end of the month I began another notebook, filling it with observations about my emotional state, questions about the accuracy of some of Dworkin's factual assertions, speculations about her personal life. I considered the conceptual strategy of overconfidence in feminist writing.

Her rhetorical certainty, the absence of apology or caveat, was calculated to defy cultural expectations of women's prose, to obliterate prettiness and deference. It was not just a decision though; it was also her gift.

I hoped that *my* gift was not the art of the apology or the caveat, the ornamental positing of my own subjective limits. I decided to be more arrogant and hyperbolic. Why not? An experiment. It'd be hard to do with my girlish voice and heart shaped lips, my desire to make money and to be liked by everyone, but nevertheless, I decided to push my feelings and ideas to their logical extremes in order to find the exact point at which they became untrue.

And thus I began to write my book about Andrea Dworkin.

Musician and writer JOHANNA FATEMAN is a founding member of the band Le Tigre and co-owner of Seagull Salon in New York.

JILL NELSON

on

ARETHA FRANKLIN

I was fourteen when Aretha's "Respect" burst out of the radio in 1967 (two years after Otis Redding, who wrote the song, released his version). I was living in that space between girlhood and young womanhood, trying to figure out how to move forward and if I really wanted to. I was surrounded by movement and movements: civil rights, antiwar, Black Power, women's, hippie. There was no respite, no space for inaction, being alive was to be necessarily embroiled. It was a heady, exhilarating, sometimes frightening time in which to come of age, a time of seemingly endless possibilities without road maps. Or at least any I could respect or intended to heed.

As a young female I was achingly aware of my physicality, my corporeal self, of the weight of my virginity as albatross and the corresponding lure of free love made possible and safe by the recent advent of birth control pills. In those turbulent times of what to a fourteen-year-old were a dizzying number of choices, many of them extreme, limbo sometimes seemed the safest place, although it was in short supply.

Then came this big, lush voice out of my pale blue transistor radio, the one I slept with under my pillow turned low and tuned to WWRL, the soul music station at the far end of the dial. The horns and funky guitar chords opening up, background singers chanting "Whoop," and then that voice I'd never heard before but was oh so familiar, an aural aspect of my molecular memory, calling out, "What you want, baby I've got it/What you need, you know I've got it/All I'm asking is for a little respect when you come home." And those women in the background chanting, "Just a little bit, just a little bit."

Oddly enough, even though Aretha Franklin's voice and the song "Respect" were new to my life, the exhortation to give "just a little bit, just a little bit" wasn't, though perhaps not in those exact words. Most often spoken in a sexual context, the meaning of those words were contradictory and confusing, could be heard as either a warning or a seduction, depending on who was doing the talking, either my mother or another female relative or my male peers or, not infrequently, older men.

I was careening into womanhood in a decade in which myriad areas of American society were being challenged, trashed, and transformed. Old norms and expectations—political, social, and cultural—were being questioned and torn down by organized and ad hoc citizens' movements. Often the only thing certain about the future direction was that it was coming on fast and would be something new. My father was largely absent, working long hours, leaving the raising of the children to my mother, a still acceptable model that was soon to be seriously reconsidered by the feminist movement. Raising three teenagers and one adolescent, my mother sought to reassure us and also slow us down. She periodically sat me and my sister, three years older, down to talk about sex. "It feels wonderful, but once you have it everything changes. Not just your relationship with the boy, but with everyone, and most of all with yourself," she cautioned. "There is no reason to rush into having sex because someone wants you to, none at all. And there is no such thing as having 'a little bit' of intercourse, whatever someone may say. But if you do decide you're ready, come to me and I will help you get birth control pills." She always added, "No questions asked."

Then there were the boys—and occasionally the predatory grown men who buzz around vulnerable young women—the ones whose eyes I could feel caress my skin when they looked at me, whose awkward kisses made me wet and ache between my legs, who I thought about when I lay in bed at night. I wasn't about to go all the way, but they didn't know that. Even so, we were headed in that direction, so with boys the ante was constantly being upped. It was always about "just a little bit" more. Let me touch your breast through your sweater, your bra, bare. Let me see the top of your titty, rub your stomach, put my hand in that hot place between your skirt and panties, let me kiss you while I'm doing all that and more. I can remember coming home sex-drunk and spinning, fondled to a fair thee well but virginity still intact, my mother's eyes looking me over hard, as if she had X-ray vision and could tell at a glance, without my saying a word, if it was time to get those birth control pills.

It was not until twenty years later, as a grown woman and the mother of a fourteen-year-old daughter myself, that I understood and appreciated the tightropes my mother was trying to help me navigate and to navigate herself, when I found myself faced with the same dilemma. How to celebrate sex without advocating for it? How to slow a young girl down without being censorious and speeding her up? How to help a daughter create positive identity in a culture simultaneously hypersexualized and puritanically judgmental about female sexuality? How to avoid being dismissed as old and irrelevant?

"Respect" was Franklin's first number one song. I heard it everywhere: on all the radios at home, wafting out the doors of the corner grocery store, filling the sidewalks, bouncing out the windows of passing cars. Aretha's voice sits at the top of the charts for months, rides the warm breezes of spring into the sweaty heat of summer in the city, East Side, West Side, Harlem, the East Village, everywhere I go Aretha is already there, welcoming, creating common ground. In the increasingly polarized last half of the 1960s, the song crossed barriers of age, class, gender, and race. The demand for respect, though subject to wide interpretation, was something we could all agree on. Who could resist the funk of Aretha's voice, Alabama's Muscle Shoals Rhythm Section, King Curtis on saxophone, and sisters Carolyn and Erma singing backup?

"Respect" was one of the few records I owned that I was allowed, even regularly invited, to play on my parents' living room stereo. I'd come home from school and my mother would ask me to play it. She'd pull the arm on the turntable back and we'd listen to that song over and over and over, at first singing along but not dancing, eventually me and my mother prancing around our staid living room, a space most often used for serious occasions or when we had company, fingers snapping, hips shaking, voices wailing as if we were Aretha. Sometimes my diminutive mother's chignon would bust loose and her thick, wavy salt-and-pepper hair would fall down past her shoulders. Music blasting, eyes closed, she didn't seem to care, just kept dancing in those high-heeled pumps she wore until she was almost eighty. I let the music take me as I watched her, danced with eyes open, for that brief time not feeling awkward, alien, or angst. "Respect" pulled my mother and me together for two minutes, twenty-eight seconds of rare and precious communion at an age and in a time when my ascent into womanhood, into adulthood, often seemed dependent on my denying any common ground.

"Respect" is a song about a relationship, and, crucially important for me, about a woman's right to negotiate from a position of power the terms of that relationship in ways that are mutually satisfying. The song made it plain that along with flirtatiously promising to fulfill her partner's sexual desires, a woman required that her needs, sexual and otherwise, be met as well. What else but backbone-bending sex could Aretha be calling forth when she came up with the line "sock it to me," demanded in a call and response with her backup singers, that blended gospel with R&B. The confidence with which Aretha dismissively assures her lover that, "What you want, you know I've got it / What you need, you know I got it," elevates to paramount importance what she wants and needs. "Respect" is a woman throwing down the terms of the relationship. Here's what I'll give, here's what I want in return, no equivocation. In case of confusion, Franklin also added "R-E-S-P-E-C-T," vocally spelling it out to further her point.

For me the most important relationship addressed in "Respect" is a woman's relationship with herself. The song is about self-definition, about a woman acknowledging her power and her needs and outlining a pathway to an empowered identity and satisfaction, sexual and otherwise. "Respect" is a fusion of the gospel world, in which Aretha, a minister's daughter, grew up, with the insistent, sexual, secular world of the late 1960s. A bridge over troubled waters.

At a time when I was immersed in grappling with gender and sexuality and also being sexualized and objectified by others, "Respect" changed my stance from overwhelmed to empowered. It made me think about what respect is and why it matters. It helped me move away from being a girl-object and toward becoming a young woman both capable of and responsible for identifying and negotiating the elements of a pleasurable intimate encounter. In "Respect," sex isn't demure or implied, it is front, center, and up for discussion. Prior to "Respect" most R&B sung by girl groups presented either a simplistic, oddly chaste notion of love, romance, and implied sexual intimacy or a sad song in response to its demise, usually at the hand of a male cad. The lyrics of "Respect" may have said "just a little bit," but Aretha's powerful voice, underscored by the horns, guitar, and backup singers, made it clear that short ends were unacceptable. Until, that is, they are.

It is this dichotomy that makes Aretha's music both seductive and repulsive, sometimes simultaneously, a never-ending tug of war between Aretha the powerful and Aretha the victim. The fractured reflections of myself I see and hear in her mirror. It is as if Aretha Franklin is living proof of what's possible and what isn't. She articulates what it is to live at the extreme ends of the dial, that place of static where there is always either too much or too little and scant peace. Sister Aretha breaks down the extremes and leaves you stretched between the ends of the spectrum. If you choose to mitigate, moderate, find balance, you've got to figure out how to do that on your own. Aretha is a woman of extremes. It is up to her listeners to fill in the blanks.

In many ways Aretha presents as a kinda regular sister, albeit with a transcendent voice, dealing with issues common to most of us. Finding love, experiencing sexual pleasure, forming a positive identity, dealing with disappointment and rejection, having a good time—all things that may sound simple but can be incredibly difficult to achieve. Yet there is also a side of Aretha's life, hinted at but largely kept silent and secret, that is deeply troubling. Abandonment, loss of childhood, early sexual activity, and possibly abuse run through Franklin's history—issues that are not atypical in many families. Franklin's lifelong reticence and secretiveness about revealing anything about her personal life is also common in troubled families.

Franklin grew up in an illustrious family in Detroit, Michigan, headed by the Reverend C. L. Franklin, a civil rights activist who, in addition to a popular radio ministry, pastored the New Bethel Baptist Church, a congregation that boasted four thousand members years before the concept of a mega-church became part of the religious, economic, and political landscape. It was a house full of music and people, a place where Sam Cooke, Dinah Washington, Jackie Wilson, or Mahalia Jackson might well drop by, the place where Aretha put down gospel roots and developed her love for secular music.

It was also the house Aretha's mother fled when Aretha was six, taking her son from a previous relationship and leaving the four children she conceived with Reverend Franklin, when she discovered her husband had impregnated a twelve-year-old parishioner. Barbara Siggers Franklin, a pianist and singer, moved to Buffalo, and Aretha visited her until she was ten and her mother died of a heart attack. With her mother gone and the Reverend Franklin busy saving souls, it fell on a grandmother and family friends to run the household and raise the children, a situation doubtless complicated by a steady stream of visitors and Aretha's talent and precociousness.

Before she was seventeen, Franklin was the mother of

two sons. It has long been rumored that her eldest son, Clarence, was fathered by a close family member, although Franklin has never named the father of either of her two oldest sons. Whoever fathered her children, Aretha was a young girl of thirteen, fourteen, or fifteen during both her pregnancies, and the relationships, incestuous or not, must have been difficult for her, a motherless child and the daughter of a famous minister and public citizen. Her demand for "Respect" was a call from the heart that rang so true when I was fourteen, around the age Aretha was when her childhood abruptly ended. Not unlike Franklin's own experience, her sons were raised by friends, as Franklin, a teenaged single parent, pursued a recording career.

In later years she married twice and had two other sons by different men, but her relationships have been short-lived and reportedly tumultuous. A chain smoker for many years, Franklin is alleged to have abused alcohol, and her relationship with food is clearly problematic—each ways to self-medicate and insulate. Most visible is her struggle with her weight. She gains, loses, gains, unable to find a physical space within which she is both comfortable and healthy, wrapping herself in protective layers that she sheds and replaces as needed.

Perhaps symbolically, she has long had a fear of flying that has negatively impacted her ability to tour widely, a phobia both ironic and revealing for a woman with such a soaring voice. No doubt Franklin's own experiences of trauma and adversity, and her capacity to survive them, contribute to her adeptness at so powerfully articulating both vulnerability and strength.

Whether it is the public Franklin singing "Precious Lord" at the funeral of Dr. Martin Luther King, Jr. after his assassination in 1968, or the private Aretha watching the slow death of her father, shot in his home by a burglar in 1979 and comatose until he died in 1984, or the public/private Aretha gaining and losing hundreds of pounds over five decades, loss has been a constant presence in Franklin's life and music.

Over the years Franklin can fade, go silent, then suddenly reappear with a fabulous album like 1985's "Who's Zoomin' Who?," or blow everyone away singing opera when she fills in for her friend Luciano Pavarotti at the Grammy Awards in 1998, or remind us who's Queen when she is named number one on *Rolling Stone*'s list of the one hundred greatest singers of all time, or a year later sing "My Country 'Tis of Thee" at Barack Obama's inauguration in that fabulous, gray, bejeweled bow with a hat attached. (She actually made "My Country 'Tis of Thee" sound believable, albeit temporarily.) That hat now lives in the Smithsonian.

Known for canceling concerts, in 2010 there were rumors that Franklin was ill with pancreatic cancer. When she emerged months later alive, apparently well, and eighty-five pounds lighter, some guessed she'd had gastric bypass surgery. Franklin denied both rumors, did not explain, and soon after announced her intention to marry her longtime companion, William Wilkerson. It was vintage Aretha when the wedding—but not the relationship, apparently—was called off a few weeks later.

The magic is that every time she waxes and wanes she leaves her music with us, a catalogue that weaves through the last half of the twentieth century, an inescapable voice in the soundtrack of many lives. Like so many of us, Franklin does not seem to have been able to get it right, and not for lack of trying.

Here in the city where I live, lying in bed on a hot summer night, the windows wide open, with the breeze and bleating car horns wafting in, here she comes too, flung from the sunroof of a car waiting for a green light ten stories below, demanding that I tell her who's zoomin' who, making me wish I too had a man named Dr. Feelgood. Like all great love affairs, my relationship with Aretha has always been intense, whether off or on. I have spent months and years listening to Aretha, then not listening to her at all, then selectively listening to a specific period of Aretha's music, then setting my iPod to "All Songs," then back to not listening at all (you get the pattern). Some, none, gimme all, take her away, encore—Aretha's music has been a lifelong relationship, a love affair I often couldn't commit to or do without, a double mirror reflecting the strongest, most independent, smartest, definitely grown-up aspects of me, then flipping to show the vulnerable, scared, hungry, hungry-for-love-and-affirmation part of me that is better denied or sublimated in order to survive intact. It is these contradictions that make Aretha so seductive and frightening, that, depending on the needs and circumstances of a particular year, day, moment can make her the voice of liberated empowerment or broke down heartache, with a sultry dose of lust thrown in.

Aretha sings into existence a universe in which the pitfalls are many but the possibilities are endless. Her voice creates a world in which I can be vulnerable, sexy, voracious, smart, demanding, powerful, and no less a woman, no less attractive for it. That her music is funky, danceable, with great lyrical hooks, that her voice channels the interior emotional life of women and is simultaneously an exhortation, a demand, and a seduction makes her irresistible.

Recently I went to my local library in Harlem and asked the young woman at the desk if they had any books about Aretha. She looked blank. Perhaps I was speaking too softly. I increased the volume. Her eyes remained uncomprehending. No a-ha moment followed when I said Aretha Franklin. I spelled first and last name for her. Nada. I left the library empty-handed and saddened. I was raised on Aretha, raised my daughter on her. It had never occurred to me that anyone could make the transition from girlhood into young womanhood or live life as a woman without Aretha telling it like it is, was, could, and should be. Who would be this younger generation's griot? Who will tell girls the truth, that "R-E-S-P-E-C-T / find out what it means to me" is something to fight for, that lust and love and pain and heartache and dancing and power and vulnerability are not only unavoidable but to be embraced and survived if you are alive? What have I learned in the nearly half a century since "Respect" burst out of my little radio and into my soul in the spring of 1967? Lovers, gigs, friends, fame, and fortune come and go. The Queen of Soul sticks with a sister for a lifetime.

JILL NELSON is the author of the memoir *Volunteer Slavery: My Authentic Negro Experience*; the essay collection *Straight, No Chaser*; the oral history *Finding Martha's Vineyard: African Americans at Home on an Island*; and the novel *Sexual Healing*. She creates gardens in New York City and on Martha's Vineyard.

RICK MOODY

on

KAREN DALTON

1

Ἄστερες μὲν ἀμφὶ κάλαν σελάνναν/ἂψ ἀπυκρύπτοισι φάεννον
εἶδος, / ὄπποτα / πλήθοισα μάλιστα λάμπη / γᾶν [ἐπὶ πᾶσαν] /
... ἀργυρία ...

[In fact, the stars orbiting that irresistible moon / Secret away
their own luminous forms / Whenever she shines without
restraint / Upon the world entire.]

—Sappho, fragment 34

The problem with writing about Karen Dalton is the legend of Karen Dalton, which is a legend noteworthy for its gaps, its wealth of inventions, as if Karen Dalton is a fragment from some ancient papyrus into which we project ourselves.

As with many celebrated musicians of the period—the deceased musicians—the circumstances of Dalton's life and death are deeply sad. There is no mistaking the sadness of her story.

Jimi Hendrix is a musician whose death has affected the interpretation of the music itself. The nature of the death of Jimi Hendrix has somehow created an environment in which the sinewy leads of Jimi Hendrix are premonitory. The story collapses time into the music, so that the music somehow seems to take place after the death of the musician.

Jim Morrison is a musician whose death has affected the interpretation of the music itself (e.g., "Break On Through to the Other Side," or, of course, "The End"). Sometimes it is hard to feel compassion for the death of Jim Morrison because the music and its provocations seem to summon up the very demise of Morrison, who knew as much. Of our elaborate plans, the end.

Janis Joplin is a musician whose death has affected the interpretation of the music itself. Perhaps unlike the afore-mentioned cases, Janis Joplin does not seem to have an unable-to-live-in-this-world quality, although her premature death could have gone no other way, it seems (reckoning from the work), as if there were no other story for Janis Joplin. Her talent was precisely maximized.

But a better example, a good comparison, when thinking of Karen Dalton, would be Jackson C. Frank. The singer released one album in the mid-1960s during his youth in England, where he was somewhat notorious (spendthrift, supernova) and well-known to people like Sandy Denny and Al Stewart (Stewart played on his one album, *Blues Run the Game*). It was produced by Paul Simon, who was in England at the time (borrowing his "Scarborough Fair" arrangement from Martin Carthy, whom he encountered there). *Blues Run the Game* is as good a folk album as anyone made in those days.

The title song has to do with Jackson Frank's childhood, in which he was badly burned in a school fire and made some money in an insurance settlement, but could never get comfortable with the disfigurement that came as a result of the injury and seven months of recuperation. He made the record, and seemed to have a lot going for him. But Frank apparently could not get comfortable, and the second album never materialized. There were gigs in England that they say were too painful to watch, howls of discomfort from the performer, and then he vanished into obscurity.

The last recordings of Jackson C. Frank, unreleased during his lifetime, made after multiple hospitalizations, occasional homelessness, and damage from years of substance abuse, are so painful to listen to that most people would probably shrink from listening to them. Now I'm down to selling prayers on my knees—that's from "Singing Sailors." Frank can't play the guitar as well as he did when he was young. His voice is totally shot, he wheezes between lines. It's not a matter of whether "Singing Sailors" is affecting, the question is whether you are sturdy enough to make the journey.

There's Phil Ochs—earnest, politically engaged, alcoholic, suicidal.

And then there's Nick Drake . . .

2

Recently a friend who worked in the free-form radio world (it's a very small world) performed a certain experiment in which she looked for songs or audio works in her collection that were exactly 4:33 in length. This was an homage to John Cage's celebrated composition "4:33." My friend came up with a great number of interesting pieces that were the same length, and she observed that when listening to these works in the context of Cage's piece interesting things happened. Among the things that came up was "In the Evening (It's So Hard to Tell Who's Gonna Love You the Best)" from the album of the same name released by Capitol Records in 1969, by Karen Dalton. This was Dalton's first official release, and it is a very strange album, intensely still, sort of placid, as if the range of actual musical gesturing taking place is meant to be the least possible required in order to indicate the presence of music. If it were not primarily the blues, you might think this album were something that we might confine to the minimalisms of New York in the mid-1960s (and, after all, she was there then, in New York). But it is the blues, and where there is something confident and stylized and postured in the acoustic blues of the same period as construed elsewhere (by men, let's say, by Mississippi Fred McDowell on *I Do Not Play No Rock 'n' Roll*, also released in 1969), in Dalton's version, the blues are so haunted and hushed that it almost seems like the blues would not be the right word for what she does. This is self-evident on "In the Evening," whose lyrics are not terribly complex. "In the evening/when the sun goes down / it's so lonesome and lonesome / when the one you love is not around." As in the blues, things get repeated twice for emphasis. The original recording is by Leroy Carr, an early blues player, who died in 1935, and who was responsible for a rather metropolitan and urbane style that had one foot in the nascent jazz tradition. And while Dalton relocates the song into the topography of the (unaccompanied) twelve-string guitar, she preserves some of the jazz feel. She phrases like a reed instrument, like a clarinet. Carr is often jaunty, almost upbeat, though his lyrics are frequently devastating (eg, "Straight Alky Blues," "Six Cold Feet In the Ground," "Suicide Blues"). He died of nephritis at thirty, so he probably came by the pain organically, and yet his blues, at least on recording, are nowhere near as distraught as Dalton's are.

Every blues singer, it seems, lays claim to the lost love trope, and Dalton is no different from Carr, but it's the gloaming part of Dalton's recording, borrowed from Carr and recast, expanded, the twilight, the diminishment of light, that is the harrowing part of Dalton's version of the song, which differs in so many respects, even in the title, as if it is bent to Dalton's purpose, where twilight is reflected in the sound of the recording, in the stillness, the radically slowed tempo, and the ache of Dalton's voice, which was already starting to give evidence of some of its creaky, gerontological qualities, so still and hushed as to be nearly silent, as though

Dalton had some knowledge of the John Cage composition, and her voice unaccompanied in a way that is perfect for the solitude of the lyric (probably there are some blues which can only be performed properly in solitude).

The other thing that is remarkable about Dalton's version of the song is that the "It's So Hard to Tell Who's Going to Love You the Best" part of the song, which goes on to become the title of the album, is entirely Dalton's invention, and is in no way integral to Carr's composition. What does the line mean? Does it mean that there are always going to be multiple lovers, which certainly was a trope of the bluesman, and an idea that would have had some currency in the freewheeling amorous counterculture of 1969? Was it an appropriation of polyandry on Dalton's part, to counterpose against the polygamy of the masculine blues? Does it mean that there is an obligation to compare the multiple lovers in order to verify the relative merits of these multiple lovers? I hew toward the "hard to tell" part of the formulation. The blues in this view is a form given to skepticism, given to negation, and in this case given to negation about belief and certainty, in which the loss of love is more as a result of the intellectual skepticism or nihilism of the thinking subject in the blues narrative. It *is* hard to tell, after all, though the song, as a trace of self, exists as a contrary affirmation.

In the same way, the Cage composition, "4:33," is skeptical about what is knowable in the field of composition, all the certainties of musical composition are removed, until the very acting of removal becomes the composition. In the final moment, Cage's silent piece recognizes its own skepticism even about silence. Silence is a space to which you aspire. There is no silence, just the yearning for silence. Dalton's first album, *It's So Hard to Tell Who's Going to Love You the Best*, similarly, is an album about stripping away, and it's partly about that because she probably didn't have a huge recording budget, because she was a woman in a man's world (there were fewer of these in 1969), but also because she was an artist coming from a traditional idiom—the folk music world—in which you didn't write your own songs, but interpreted the classics that were all around you. And also because stripping away brings the impulse of the blues into focus, allows you to see into the blues, allows affirmation through formal transparency. The fact that in 1969 the blues was, almost uniformly, a form given to men seems to animate Dalton's impulse, as though Dalton remakes the idiom. Her version takes silence and twilight as models for how to talk about loss, and they are evoked in the very simple picking patterns of her twelve-string, and in the microtonal richness of her voice (which is where the Billie Holiday comparison seems to come from), the faint end-of-the-line vibrato, and the overtones. A woman singing the blues. This is what it's supposed to sound like, and there's no mistaking that *It's So Hard to Tell Who's Going to Love You the Best* is an album of the blues, largely played solo or in small ensembles by a woman, in the year of Altamont, Woodstock, the last performance of the Beatles, the last performance of the Jimi Hendrix Experience, etc. As such, entirely revolutionary.

3

The facts are incomplete. First, there is the matter of Enid, Oklahoma, where all accounts say Dalton was born and raised. It's the ninth-largest city in Oklahoma, equidistant between Tulsa and Wichita, Kansas, pretty much in the middle of a large expanse of agricultural land, and is designated the wheat capital of Oklahoma (and also the Purple Martin capital of Oklahoma), though these days it also features oil and gas production, and is now somewhat beholden to fracking to the point where north of Enid there have been some of those ominous mini-earthquakes that are associated with this recent type of extraction.

The facts are incomplete as to the particulars of Dalton's family, except that she was of Cherokee derivation (her own daughter disputes this), whether in part or in full is obscure, and the main thrust of her early biography as it is known is that Dalton was exceedingly musical, and that this was of some note to her mother. Any account in public by Dalton's children is vague as to her paternity. The early biography is bent by the gravitational yank of the music, and thus when people assert that Dalton's biography is somehow "more folk" than the biographies of others on the scene, they are talking about the music. All of this, in a way, is shit, is the talk of what genuineness is, and the genuine is the most dangerous drug of all, and in the maw of the genuine many musicians had been lain waste. That said, Dalton grew up in the expanses of the Great Plains, and she was part of the oppressed class, if by oppressed you mean the group of people subjected to genocide (if, at least, there is validity to the Cherokee interpretation) and she sang, early on, the traditional music, and she left Enid to come east, with her child, or her children, and who can blame her.

You could argue that the second the traditional music leaves the Great Plains, the music becomes less traditional and more postmodern, more experimental, the site of appropriation by a class of educated music aficionados who are less adequate to the appreciation of its tradition.

Her "real" name was Karen J. Cariker, and in no instance have I been able to account for the J. It seems to be a placeholder for a middle name, or for a tradition of middle names. I also have been unable to locate the person or persons who supplied Dalton with the surname "Dalton," and since it was appropriated later by Lacey J. Dalton in honor of Karen Dalton, who was a friend, landlady, and "student" of Karen Dalton, it's as if the name Dalton is always appropriated and never exists on its own, standing in, perhaps, for the way surnames were once swapped in and out for women.

Dalton arrived in New York in the late 1950s or early 60s, in either case for the tail end of everything beatnik, as well as the beginning of the American folk revival as it was being played out on college campuses. The exact date of her arrival is again, subject to debate, and indicates the sketchiness of the facts. A biography of Dalton that is a stable and interpretation-free narrative of Dalton is impossible. The matter of relocation—whether more Beat or more civil rights era—has some bearing on how we think about Dalton and her recorded work. A Beat Dalton is not coming to New York because of the flowering of coffeehouses because between 1955 and 1959, folk music was in part driven underground by the witch-huntery of the House Un-American Activities Committee, which had fingered Pete Seeger and Lee Hays (of The Weavers) as subversives, affecting their own professional livelihoods and branding, to some extent, this music as leftist. The situation didn't really change until the success of the Kingston Trio, the New Christy Minstrels, et al. But a Karen Dalton who arrived later would not be as motivated by the labor union part of the folk canon, nor by the legendary voices of that early part of the folk tradition, and yet she certainly was schooled in these things.

Peter Walker, a Cambridge-based folk musician and guitar innovator (in the Sandy Bull or John Fahey way of things) knew Dalton well, and speaks of meeting her first in 1961 with her husband of the time, Richard Tucker: ". . . slick New York cool casual clothes, and an air of confidence and nobility. They knew who they were, they were on a mission."* Dalton was twenty-four in 1961, which suggests that Dalton's move to New York happened early enough for her to get to the city and acquire a look, a persona, a collaborator, and so on, in order to be performing in Cambridge by 1961.

*Peter Walker, *Karen Dalton: Songs, Poems, and Writings,* (Woodstock, NY: Ark Press, 2013), 2.

She had also already been married twice, and had (if I am assembling the conflicting reports properly), two children. In short, a whole life in Oklahoma had been cast off, and a new one begun.

4

A version of the folk narrative that is more Beat era and less civil rights era, more Lead Belly and less Joan Baez, would perhaps include some more permissive attitudes about narcotics.

It's impossible to address the biography of Karen Dalton without speaking to the issue of narcotics. Many of the men on the folk scene that Dalton knew well (and whose songs she eventually interpreted), had significant association with narcotics. Tim Hardin (whose "Reason to Believe," Dalton covered during her lifetime, and which can be heard in a stunning rendition on *1966*, a home-recorded rehearsal tape of Dalton and, it is said, a soon-to-be-estranged husband Richard Tucker) died of an overdose. Fred Neil, one of the godfathers of the scene (along with Dave Van Ronk), was not free of the demon, nor can it be said of others along the way, like David Crosby, or Peter Stampfel. It was part of the milieu of folk music, and the ethos of heroin was the ethos of Beat in the late 1950s. Heroin was part of the experience, part of the jazz demimonde, wherein almost no major player didn't have his or her struggle with narcotics. The question of why heroin was so prevalent is beyond the bounds of these pages, but it was an evocation of the doomed blues of the early folk scene—a questionable evocation of liberty, of self-determination—but also a kind of backward testament to the cost of living in these songs, as though the songs themselves are hard on the practitioners.

If Dalton was "slick New York cool," she also carried around the Cherokee lineage (perhaps) and Dust Bowl authenticity, and the general desperation of being a woman trying to make it in a scene that was only beginning to have women in it (Joan Baez and Judy Collins being standard bearers). These factors could all account for the attraction to the oblivion of narcotics for Dalton. It also helps force the inevitable comparison to Billie Holiday, a comparison that, by some accounts, Dalton disdained. Holiday, like Dalton, became entangled with the problem of addiction, and like Dalton, died of it. (There is also, it bears mentioning, the register each of them sang in—that reedy alto—and also the lazy, relaxed-to-the-point-of-offhanded phrasing that each of them affected, in which the affect was in the song and the words, and the willingness to be quiet—you can't overstate how important dynamics, and, in particular, quietness is to the greatness of Karen Dalton. The material may have been different. That is, Holiday was certainly a jazz singer. But that's about the only thing that Holiday and Dalton didn't have in common. The way the ravages of time played into their later recordings is similar. And the sense of the blues that you get from being a non-white musician in a white-dominated music conglomerate.)

The people who recorded Dalton when she made her albums often speak to the role of narcotics in her recordings—Harvey Brooks said he'd never seen her when heroin was not involved. And she did die of HIV. In Peter Walker's compendium of her poems and diaries there is a significant amount of allusion to the burden of narcotics.

Heroin may have been part of music culture in the 50s. Heroin may have been part of the noble savagery of the folk music world, written between its verses as some testament to the kind of difficulties (murder, loss, romance, destitution) described therein. Heroin may have been part of Dalton's vulnerability personally. But that doesn't stop you from wishing it were otherwise.

5

The beauty of Karen Dalton also gets in the way of a discussion of the music of Karen Dalton, which is what this essay is about, not the singer's life but the singer's songs. The question might be rephrased thus: What do we mean by the beauty of Karen Dalton? Are we speaking of the physical appearance of Karen Dalton? Do we know what we mean by the appearance of Karen Dalton? Does the physical beauty of the singer have an effect on the interpretation of the songs? And the related inquiry is: What is the relationship of this white male music critic, the writer of these pages, to the question of the beauty of Karen Dalton? If a libidinous attachment to Dalton is what drives the legend of Karen Dalton, can I, the writer of these pages, entirely uncathect from the legend of Karen Dalton in order to arrive at, it is to be hoped, a critical detachment to see what's good here, what's valuable, without getting clotted up by a purely or primarily romanticized construction of the singer?

My story is as follows: a friend of mine played "Something On Your Mind" for me at a dinner party not so long after the Karen Dalton reissue phenomenon began to gather up its head of steam. I had read about Karen Dalton, at that point, but had not yet heard her. I am only a distant admirer of that tendency, in record-collecting circles, to hunt the great neglected classic, Judee Sill, let's say, or Vashti Bunyan, or Terry Callier. And yet I was, it bears saying, incredibly moved by hearing "Something On Your Mind." I became instantly obsessed with the song, in exactly the way I delight in being musically obsessed.

Since childhood, I have had these obsessive fainting spells, these moments of hysteria. Some other examples of them would be: "Sloop John B.," by the Beach Boys (1966), "Something," by the Beatles (1969), "Black Dog," by Led Zeppelin (1971), "Accidents Will Happen," by Elvis Costello and the Attractions (1979), "Because the Night," Patti Smith (1978), and so on. It would be worth an investigation into the specific nature of that experience of fastening onto a song, and the ways in which a fastening onto a song is different from sudden paralytic romantic need. I think with the Beach Boys song it had to do with the phrase "I wanna go home," which is repeated several times. Some emotional need, some need for a specific emotional articulation, can reside in a song, regardless of the specific lyrical trajectory of the song ("Something" by the Beatles, for example, resists easy lyrical interpretation, so what was it in "Something" that was so attractive to my nine-year-old self?).

When you need to hear the song, what is it you need to hear? As the critic David Grubbs has asked, why do you need to hear it again and again? It's a socially sanctioned example of repetition compulsion. As the tendency on my part has often adhered to songs I found *embarrassing*, or even moronic ("Back In Black," by AC/DC, let's say), it is not necessarily always the value of the song itself that causes this fastening to happen. Nor is the attractiveness of the singer a part of this feeling (I have never considered Don Van Vliet attractive, though I am overpowered by his music, and the same is true of John Lydon, Courtney Love, Sun Ra, Frank Zappa, Stephin Merritt, La Monte Young), though sometimes the fastening-on engenders feelings that are related to the appreciation of beauty in their intensity.

In the Karen Dalton case, I loved the song, but I did not, in truth, pay much attention to the physical condition of the singer in photographs. Indeed, I didn't see them at first. The photographs, which, as I argue below, are misleading, nearly intentionally so, corresponded to and were coincident for me with some horror about the facts of the biography, which I soon began to uncover in the process of learning more.

My particular obsession with Dalton, which needs to be of a certain cast in order to produce English-language prose, quickly transcended both the physical facts about Dalton and the legends associated with her biography, and, as I argue later, the obsession became coincident with the voice itself. Can one cathect emotionally onto a purely sonic or auditory phenomenon? My obsession with the sound of Dalton's voice may not be libidinous but it is tangentially related, in that I have a slightly exaggerated belief in the expressive power of the sound of the voice of the singer, and this belief finds its expression only in the recordings by Karen Dalton, not in the facts of the now-deceased person by the same name.

There are a few photographs, and they seem expert at capturing Dalton in a certain way, a certain kind of meditative and downcast pose that seemed, in the 60s, to indicate artistic seriousness (even artists who weren't so meditative and melancholy were often posed in this way). There is for example the famous photograph of Dalton, Bob Dylan, and Fred Neil gigging at the Café Wha? (1961), in which Dalton appears to be belting it out in a manner that is at some variance with her reputation for extremes of quiet. I think there is another reason this photograph persists, and it does not have to do with the argument that Dalton is a perpetual libidinous object of the male musicians of the scene. I think this photograph is reproduced a lot because it's one of the rare photographs of Karen Dalton in which she has all of her teeth.

Sometime in the mid-60s, as has been noted by one of Dalton's children, Abralyn Baird, Dalton lost a couple of teeth getting in the middle of a fight between romantic partners: "The man she was living with at the time, he came home and found her in bed with my soon-to-be stepfather. . . She got punched in the face. She always said when she got that big recording contract and became famous, she was gonna have teeth put in."* The absence of teeth becomes part of the story thereafter, and when Lacy J. Dalton, in the 90s, intervenes and persuades Karen Dalton to check into a rehabilitation facility (so this particular story goes), likewise to get her teeth fixed, Dalton bails out, and refuses the dentistry in order to continue to procure codeine for her presumably significant dental pain. In any event, no photograph after the early 60s exists without her trying to conceal the missing teeth, and, as a result, there are very few photographs of Dalton smiling.

There are very few photos of her at all, but the absence of a smile is a feature of those that do exist. There are two commercially available videos of Dalton performing (the better of which is of "It Hurts Me Too" from her first album).† The second of these ("Blues Jumped the Rabbit") has

*"Karen Dalton: A Reluctant Voice Rediscovered," by Joel Rose, Morning Edition, National Public Radio, July 12, 2008, 6:00 AM.
†http://www.youtube.com/watch?v=H0ZIWK-b_KY

some footage of her in the kitchen and out in the Colorado woods, retrofitted, it seems, with an earth mother interpretation. Each of these is notable for the missing teeth. "Blues Jumped the Rabbit" has a close-up of Dalton smiling, and it is much more complex for including this moment.

The beauty of Dalton is an effect of the music, in some ways, and all the legends that spring up (like the Cherokee legend), seem to be a way to attempt to describe the music as much as they are ways of describing Dalton herself. That the still camera managed to find and capture Dalton by misrepresenting her complexity is not unusual. Whereas in other cases a fair amount of technological manipulation is required in photographic misrepresentation, in Dalton's case it's different. She just had to look down. And all at once there she was, the stunningly beautiful alleged Cherokee, who was demure and thoughtful, and not the person, as her daughter remarks, who would yell at a bank teller. So the biography of Dalton up to the time of her commercially released albums, the ones with which she cooperated, *It's So Hard to Tell Who's Going to Love You the Best* (1969) and *In My Own Time* (1971), is full of half-truths, misrepresentations, and the kind of freely invented material that we associate with the folk tradition. As if Dalton's life were of the songs rather than separate from the songs. For every reliable source (Richard Tucker saying Dalton's father was a chronic alcoholic) there is another disagreeing entirely (often Dalton's daughter Abralyn Baird).

6

μφί μοι αὖτις ἄναχθ᾽ ἐκατηβόλον ἀειδέτω φρήν

[Anew, for me in the heavenly trajectory of the gods, there is my music…]

—Terpander, fragment 2

Terpander is the Greek musician whose lines are often referred to by other Greeks but in a way so fragmentary that it's not certain whether he wrote any of these words, nor is it certain whether he really meant that he was responsible for adding three strings to the lyre so that it had seven instead of four, and his particular accomplishment is that he was a simplifier and popularizer of Greek musical styles that were happening around him. Part of his reputation rests on the fact of the music itself, and the legend adheres to the fact of the music. Terpander may not exist at all, or not in the way that he appears to exist according to later exegetes, and the same difficulties seem to adhere to Karen Dalton. This is especially the case when you listen to her recordings. Part of the problem, in fact, is recording itself. It has been observed (by Greil Marcus, notably) that the bootlegs by Bob Dylan are better than the official releases, and this has often been the case with the music of the early folk period, that its relationship to electronic tape has been more antagonistic than comfortable.

Dalton, for all her confidence and certainty about who

she was as a musician, seemed to blanch when the tape machine began to roll. Numerous posthumous recordings by Karen Dalton are either rehearsal tapes or instances when Dalton was being recorded without her knowledge, and they do seem to memorialize a less tortured result. Of the two releases that Dalton permitted and collaborated on, there are any number of problems of which we might speak. The first, *It's So Hard to Tell Who's Going to Love You the Best*, is the better, using acoustic guitar and twelve-string acoustic, instruments that were close to Dalton's heart (she seems to have played twelve-string and long-necked banjo on almost all occasions in public). The rhythm section on *It's So Hard to Tell* approaches the blues as though they had a lot in common with jazz. The drums are so unobtrusive as to be nearly absent when there at all. The album leans hard on the blues, which Fred Neil noted was one of Dalton's strongest suits ("She sure can sing the shit out of the blues"). And the tempos are slow, which is one of Dalton's signatures as well. Sometimes the tempos feel almost opiated, and Dalton's delivery lacks the urgency that you hear, for example, on *Cotton Eyed Joe*, a live recording from 1962. The 1962 recording feels more traditional, with Dalton having more of the Appalachian about her. *It's So Hard to Tell* wipes away the high lonesome of the Karen Dalton of 1962 and replaces it with the slightly glassy-eyed desperations of Dalton's Billie Holiday-ish later work. Fred Neil's "Blues On the Ceiling" is particularly beautiful here.

Of what would a good Caucasian singer of the blues consist? Generally, we imagine that a good white blues singer, an Eric Clapton, let's say, or a Greg Allman, has a particularly good sense of the musicality of blues phrasing, knows where a note bends, knows how Robert Johnson bends it, how Howlin' Wolf howls. White blues singers are students of the blues. But a separate school of thought has it that to sing the blues you have to pay the dues, you have to, like Pierre Menard trying to rewrite Cervantes, require the expression of the blues, and that doesn't mean, you know, that you sang in a lot of clubs, and you let the amazing black bluesman at the top of the bill throw a few crumbs of enlightenment your way, the amazing bluesman who has the whole three hundred years of African-American oppression at his back as he commences to investigate his form. The white blues singers, in this view, rarely are capable of playing the blues, can't do it, can't believe in the way you have to believe in order to spontaneously produce, let's say, "Suicide Blues," or "Hard Time Killing Floor Blues," or "Crawlin' Kingsnake."

One argument might be, in fact, that a woman is more capable of feeling the kind if disenfranchisement that makes it possible to sing the shit out of the blues, that the disenfranchisement of a woman is more than perfectly adequate, but the industry, or a confluence of oppressive forces including the industry, have kept them down. Thus, there's something uncanny happening with Dalton's blues on *It's So Hard to Tell*, and it doesn't have to do with the opiates and the alcohol and the missing teeth and the manifold woes—these seem to be by-products of the kind of insight that is necessary in order to produce this slowed down, haunted, dynamically muted blues, this 3 a.m. blues, this tried-to-kidnap-her-daughter blues, this fell-out-of-the-music-business blues, this Billie Holiday vibrato applied to the blues. Dalton has something, and not many white singers had it. She lived the blues in the way necessary to produce spontaneously this peculiarly American variant on West African music. She has access to this material, so if she's not "full-blooded Cherokee" on her mother's side, she somehow has access to the oppression in the way that few Caucasian singers do.

7

Whatever *It's So Hard to Tell* is (with its epistemological uncertainty right out there in the title), it is a significantly better album than *In My Own Time*. This second album unites Dalton with a great musical director (Harvey Brooks, who as is often noted, played on both *Highway 61 Revisited* and *Bitches Brew*), who also appeared on her first album. Brooks may have been a trusted ally but he can't seem to resist the temptation to arrange. True, the album has the most gorgeous Dalton recordings extant, if that is what you're after. Dino Valenti's "Something On Your Mind," which opens, is stately, gorgeous, and ominous. And then there are a few other gems, like "Same Old Man," which is spooky and perfect, with faint traces of droning in the rear of the mix, while Dalton plays banjo and sings in a way that has more to do with the Carter Family than it has to do with Billie Holiday. Brooks can't get in the way of the song and the singer, in this case, as he even manages to do elsewhere, even on "Katie Cruel," Dalton's signature tune, which doesn't have pedal steel or horns, but it does have an intrusive fiddle. (The alternate mix on the reissue, with some old-style whistling in a lower key is an improvement.)

Everything in the Karen Dalton career, the career that took place while she was alive, turns on the song "Katie Cruel." *It's So Hard to Tell* is the only album that doesn't have a recording of "Katie Cruel" on it. So there are five recordings of the song available as of the time of writing these lines. The song performs the modal trick of lots of old-time banjo music, never quite leaves its home key, its one chord, and, for all that, manages to permit a melody at once austere, grim, and very beautiful. The "When I first came to town" mnemonic structure of the story, in which the narrator is depleted of all that is good (she goes from "roving jewel" to "Katie Cruel"), is familiar enough in the Old-Time songbook. But there are some rather haunting and philosophical turns in the song too: "If I was where I would be / Then I'd be where I am not / Here I am where I must be / Where I would be, I cannot." In the course of the many recordings of "Katie Cruel," this little chorus goes from being a vague, oblique statement about love to something much more grand and generalized, a statement about the condition of the singer herself, who comes to identify with it somehow, where Katie is Karen (and renamed as such in a Richard Manuel song from *The Basement Tapes*, "Katie's Been Gone"). You can feel her learning the song, living the song, becoming the song. The *Cotton Eyed Joe* recording from 1962 is on acoustic guitar and it sounds rushed and somehow incomplete. (And Karen Dalton almost never rushes anything.) The *Green Rocky Road* recording is on banjo and nearly twice as long as any other recording of it, and Dalton takes her time with the drone of the thing for minutes before beginning singing. The *1966* version is perfect, slow, in the slightly higher key, and Dalton's voice is confident in reaching for it. And then there are the two versions from the *In My Own Time* sessions. For me, the alternate version reprises, if in a lower key, the *1966* version, but Dalton's voice sounds weary, uncertain, and the skepticism, the annihilation, the almost theological uncertainty of the chorus, it feels premonitory, as if the singer knows that her recording career (and the dental care that might have come with it) is about to end.

In America, it bears mentioning, the song has been sung since Revolutionary War times, but the earliest American "Katie Cruel" is more of a love song than is Dalton's version, "I know who I love/And I know who does love me . . ." Dalton's chorus appears only once in the original, so the refrain of the composition is all her own. Her "Katie Cruel" is all before/after, all alcohol and unstated loss. That this version of "Katie Cruel" is gussied up on *In My Own Time* is the evidence of that album's mixed results. For me it's an album of its moment: 1971. Its reliance on well-known songs like "How Sweet It Is to Be Loved By You" and "When A Man

Loves A Woman" is disappointing (as if the material were selected by committee), and the arrangements threaten to overwhelm Dalton's voice. Given that quietness is the dynamic feature of this singer, filling in the space must, and does, muffle some of the dynamic accomplishments that are so singular to her. The problems for me are analogous to the problems with Nick Drake. *Pink Moon* is overpowering in part because there's nowhere for the singer to hide, and the space in the recording, which is all guitar and voice, lets the songs live and breathe. Dalton, like Drake, started in the folk scene, was a bona fide voice of the folk revival in New York City, and if she had been treated in the recording studio as if she were that folk singer, then there would be a lot more great recorded material by her, assuming—and this is a big if—she could ever get comfortable in front a microphone. This is why the bootleg recordings now seeing the light of day (all of them recorded on technology fifty years old) are so much better than the official releases. No ornament.

8

The story is that *In My Own Time* is called what it's called because Dalton couldn't finish anything, and wasn't well, and even if she could finally do multiple takes, she didn't like the results (her daughter is insistent on this point) and wasn't in control of her product. The attempts to tour and perform after the record was released were not much better. On some occasions, it seems, she refused to come out onstage. The story feels not unlike some of those myths of Chan Marshall (of Cat Power), and her tendency to walk off a stage (during early performances) for all of her vulnerability.

In My Own Time does occasionally feel as though Dalton is singing on a different record from the one on which Harvey Brooks's no-hair-out-of-place band is playing. As with *It's So Hard to Tell*, part of the miracle of *In My Own Time* is that it has been rescued at all, as it is more a valedictory by Dalton—her last attempt to crack the record business—than it is an installment in a career. (As such, "Are You Leaving for the Country" is a just farewell—Dalton back on her twelve-string, on a song written by her third husband Richard Tucker, with no rhythm section at all, the arrangement not unlike some of the earliest recordings, and less like the overproduced tracks on the rest of the album. Probably the song refers to the retreat in Colorado that Tucker and Dalton shared, either emblematically or actually. And Dalton's voice on the last track is much more vulnerable and mixed forward).

Her own time, her subjective time, turned out to be so attenuated, so outside of the rigors of time as we normally experience it, probably something more like heroin-addict time, in which a lot of the major decisions and their consequences can be put off a little longer. There is no major recording by Karen Dalton after *In My Own Time*, at all, for the final twenty-two or so years remaining in her life, though Nicholas Hill, who was responsible in a large measure for the reissues that brought Karen Dalton back from the brink, says that there were perhaps recordings in the 1970s with the Holy Modal Rounders (whose Steve Weber is responsible for the arrangement of "Same Old Man" that is a high point of *In My Own Time*). Lacy J. Dalton, the "student" and one-time landlady of Dalton, attempted to get Karen Dalton back into the studio in the early 90s without success. Of course, as in all such mythologies, the reissues came after the death of the artist.

9

One of the reasons Dalton never made much money from her recorded legacy during her lifetime is that she never really wrote any of the songs, not in the way that we think about songwriting in the late 60s and 70s. Fred Neil and Tim Hardin certainly wrote, were even prolific for a time. But there was a completely different idea of songwriting that dates to the folk revival, and in that idea of songwriting all of the good songs have already been composed, and your responsibility is simply to inhabit, to make the songs again for the contemporary audience. Even interpretation in this sense is an excess of intervention in the song (and this is perhaps another superficial difference between Billie Holiday and Karen Dalton)—in the folk revival you are meant to vanish into the material. Look at, for example, the tradition of Irish fiddle music: generations of fiddlers sawing away at those jigs and reels, with varieties of phrasing and intonation that, in the main, only other fiddlers can truly understand. The singer, in this traditional song, is an effect of the song, not vice versa, and yet Dalton, who completely rearranged and recalibrated songs to her own purpose ("In the Evening" on *It's So Hard To Tell*, or "Katie Cruel," or "Same Old Man"), did disappear into the songs, and while she might have been a difficult human being, whatever that implies, as a singer her wispy end-of-line vibrato and her clarinet-ish voice on the major recordings are the presence of her absence. Dalton is the least evident remainder of a singer in the history of these songs. Everything about her is subtle, and that may be why Dalton was destined to have a faint impact during her lifetime.

But what's odd about this system of choices is that others coming from a similar direction managed to parlay the same origins into massive commercial success. I'm thinking not only of Bob Dylan, but also of A. P. Carter of the Carter Family, who was as much of a genius of copyright as Bill Gates was, by synthesizing Appalachian and country music that he heard happening around him, and copyrighting many of the songs in his own name, with only minor interventions in music or lyrics. In the Carter Family, Sara and Maybelle, who were much more responsible for the sound of the recordings (Maybelle's guitar sound is the very bedrock of country music, and Sara was the lead vocalist on the great majority of Carter Family recordings), somehow failed to capitalize on the publishing and their decision to keep touring and recording long after A. P. had retired is perhaps demonstrative of the fact that they had to profit from the performances because they could not profit from the Carter Family recordings. Like Maybelle and Sara, Dalton failed to write, or failed to wrest control of the traditional songs in her direction (Joan Baez had the same problems), whether from inclination or from some sense of the tradition of traditional music is impossible to pinpoint from hindsight.

10

Dalton's later years are as hard to account for as her early life. There seem to be two principle sources for these disparate narratives. One is the aforementioned Lacy J. Dalton (she has a great variety of opinions in one *Guardian* article on the subject). And one is Peter Walker, who was well acquainted with Dalton upstate, in the Woodstock era, during her eventual illness and death. The lore of these years is that Dalton was homeless, living on the street for some portion of the 80s. But Walker's heartfelt, self-published compendium of Dalton's writings (much of it gleaned, one supposes, from Dalton's effects at the time of her death) tells a different version of the story, namely that Dalton had an apartment in New York City and a place upstate for a long time and that, ultimately, she lost her apartment in the city, whether for being priced out, or for other reasons, we do not know. Coincident with this is allusion to an unknown virus that plagued her in her later years, which we now suppose to be HIV. Dalton's daughter Abralyn disputes the HIV diagnosis and says that her mother died of throat cancer. Lenny Kaye (guitarist and Nuggets-archivist) is meanwhile the source for some of the living-on-the-streets stuff, which Walker has rebuffed thus:

> Let me put to rest these ideas that she died in destitute poverty and drug addicted homelessness . . . She was perfectly functional mentally. She was living in Hurley, in upstate New York between Kingston and Woodstock. She lived with AIDS for more than eight years, but with an excellent quality of life considering the disease.*

There can be little doubt that Dalton's long-term drug abuse didn't help with her difficulties later in life (Peter Stampfel of the Holy Modal Rounders, in one interview, observed that in the late 60s Dalton shot amphetamines, and then, later in life, "like many people, she became an alcoholic"). But that doesn't account for the great profusion of myths about Dalton's post-recording biography. A very moving essay by one Mairead Case, "Karen Dalton, Roving Jewel" makes the case that part of the prismatic distortions orbiting around Dalton have to do with masculine ideas about Dalton, a kind of cathecting onto the myth of Dalton ("the

---

*"In Her Own Time: The Return of Karen Dalton," by Jim Caligiuri, *Houston Chronicle*, February 8, 2008.

men who said she was broken or witchy . . .") at the expense of the actual Dalton, whoever she was. (I hope it is obvious by now that I wish to avoid exactly this critical trap, which is the trap of paternalism, despite fervent appreciation for the vulnerability of Dalton's voice.) There seems to be truth in this hypothesis, that almost everyone who has an opinion about Dalton seems to love her in some immoderate way, whether an imaginary Dalton or an actual Dalton, though at this point the imaginary Daltons far outnumber any other. Nicholas Hill, when I asked him about the reams of disinformation about Dalton, suggested that people invent narratives about Dalton's life "because they can," because she is not about to inconvenience these inventions now. (You can see the same trajectory in the rediscoveries of Nick Drake or Gene Clark.) In this way, the reissue in the world of music becomes as suspect, as compromised by the merchandising impulse, as any initial release. The reissue requires a story, and in this case, the subject seems to have provided some of the salacious tidbits herself, as well some of the mystery and evasiveness that makes the biography seem so plunderable. The reissue requires mythmaking, and, therefore, though the reissue is part of what brings attention back to this singer, the reissue is the enemy of the singer in some ways, too. Walker's *Karen Dalton: Songs, Poems, and Writings*, is so earnest, so full of collegial feeling, and perhaps because of this it is so fragmentary and collage-like that it does much to push the mythologizing aside, in a homespun and grammatically impulsive way wherein sometimes the narrative voice submerges itself into the quotations:

> Life was not all tragedy and suffering for Karen, she laughed, she hung out, she socialized, she guided other people out of the city and into a healthy country life.

> She wrote, "He lives in the light and probable/He lives in the might and magical/He lives in the highly improbable person."*

Walker says Dalton had a job "handing out flyers" in the late 80s. He says she was a voracious reader. He says she had trouble keeping an apartment in the Bronx. Like Dalton's writings, his version of the story unfolds in fits and starts, until it gets to the dire end:

> The next day I got there about 10:30, I knocked and let my self [sic] in. Karen appeared to be sleeping. I figured she probably needed the rest and decided not to wake her for half an hour. I sat and watched the price

---

*And in case you want to hear more of her poetical voice: "What use did addiction serve / Not easing pain, it's not like most often depicted / Get hurt by lover, so get high to ease the pain / Maybe it's so subtly hooking because it's easy to / be devoted, to thrust all that misplaced love, that / spirited charade that captured shadow, to capture / to grab all to myself a mold-able flexible reinforcing / risk you can't risk."

is right [*sic*] on the TV that was in the living room next to the bed. Bob barker [*sic*] had just awarded the final showcase prizes and I knew it was coming to the end of the half hour so decided to wake Karen. I shook her shoulder but she didn't move.

The Lacy J. Dalton version and the Peter Walker version and the Abralyn Baird version of the Karen Dalton biography are at such variance from one another there is no easy way to reconcile them except to rely on the fact that all of the narrators have had reason to spin the story in the way they do. The tragedy of Karen Dalton, in this view, tells you something about the teller of the tale.

11

περὶ μεγέθους ἡλίου] εὖρος ποδὸς ἀνθρωπείου

[And now let's speak of the sun—it's the size of your foot.]
—*Heraclitus, fragment DK-B3*

And yet there was always her voice, and there will always be her voice. If the problem with a biography of Karen Dalton is the fact of fragments, then the fragments are made less fragmentary by the voice, and some of what makes the voice so moving is the degree to which it unites all the massing of stories, all the disparate and warring sentiments, into one indisputable here and now. As Gary Giddins said about Miles Davis, the surroundings of Karen Dalton may change from album to album, bootleg to bootleg, and her situation may change, based on the progress of her addictive illness, but the uncanny persuasiveness of her voice is always there, the timbre, the bell-like tone, the bright opening of each line, the falling away into vibrato at the end, the flat vowels of the plains, the slight nasal quality, the smoky edges of the voice, the tendency to start high and go low, there's the consonance of it with all the really old voices, with Appalachian singing, there's the vulnerability, the wobbly pitch that comes in startlingly confident just when you are unsure of it, there's the brashness and the weakness, the humility, there's the way her voice goes on, even though she resisted ever being recorded and viewed recording as something highly suspect. In fact, there's something timeless about this voice, and if what you want from music is that music should work its way through the frame of the song, and into the reservoir of feeling that is apart from culture, if it is the thing with music that it should reach you somewhere where even the lyrics of the song cannot reach you, then Karen Dalton's voice is one of those voices, and there are not many of those. Others began their careers with this indelible quality but they could not sustain the commitment to this kind of pure musical sensation, this fealty to the meaning of songs, and so later in their work these singers became impervious to vulnerability. Karen Dalton didn't do that, because she gave up recording so early. As a result we have what we have of her in a very pure state.

We have this voice. Sometimes it's possible to think of her as a lost cause, a casualty of the era in which she practiced, unable to make the most of what she had, but then the evidence comes back to us again, that she wasn't silent, and that in her fragmentary output, she was also incredibly certain about what she wanted, and she whittled away at what others wanted from her, trying to get back to her voice, to its interpretations, her habitations of the song.

It's up to us to try to read the facts the way she might have read them, or sang them, apart from all the talk about Karen Dalton, in the songs, in the voice. All the pretty girls gonna leave this town, won't be back till spring, I'll sing hallelujah / you'll sing hallelujah / when they arrive at home.

RICK MOODY is the author of five novels, including *The Ice Storm* and *The Four Fingers of Death*; three collections of stories; a memoir, *The Black Veil*; and a collection of essays, *On Celestial Music*. He writes regularly about music for *Salon* and *The Rumpus*, and has released three albums with The Wingdale Community Singers. He teaches writing at New York University and Yale.

HANNE BLANK

on

M.F.K. FISHER

I

Earlier in my career as a writer, I edited anthologies of erotica. You might imagine this to be a busman's holiday of a job, maybe not even so much a job for which one ought to be paid. Heaven knows enough people told me so.

What those people did not realize, and neither did I until I was mired to the neck in piles of eager submissions, is that it is a dreadful job. Trust me when I tell you that bad things happen when the average person takes a pen in one hand and genitals in the other. Spelling and grammar and punctuation and usage get battered and scattered in the headlong scramble for climax, of course, but that's actually not what makes it miserable, just unintentionally hilarious.

What makes it miserable is the banality, the oversimplification, the lack of perception, the failure to look beyond the paint-by-numbers groaning to find any of the deeper significance of sex.

Wading through vast bogs of bad sex writing gave me the creeping horrors. Custom could, in fact, stale sex's infinite variety and wilt the hard-on of the mind. The badly written, unreflective, thoughtless sex writing of the slush piles was worse. A scant few books' worth of erotica-editing later, I retired from the fray. I still write about sex. It still fascinates me. Now, however, I do it as a historian.

I have not yet, however, escaped the experience of venturing to read about one of life's great pleasures and being bludgeoned into an unresponsive stupor by the thoughtless, the banal, and the axe-to-grind extremism of those who believe that possession of a normally functioning body plus the ability to compose sentences means they must have something worthy to share.

I refer to food writing, and to much of contemporary food media. From celebrity chefs to the rank-and-file who supply Tony Bourdain with Ray-Bans and Rolaids, our infamously confessional culture has wandered into the kitchen of the pop-cultural party and refuses to leave.

Our food experiences are of course meaningful to us. But unless we can dissect and discuss their meaning as well as the simple fact of the experiences, obsessively documenting them creates little value to anyone except perhaps far-future historians looking for documentary evidence of the foodways of twenty-first-century narcissists with disposable income.

Yet we do it in hordes, whether anyone asks us to or not. The urge has always been with us—as the great Brillat-Savarin wrote, "The single word *gastronomy* makes everyone prick up his ears. The subject is always fashionable. And mockers like to eat, as well as the rest!"—and the Internet has made it instantaneously available. But Brillat-Savarin also wrote, "Tell me what you eat and I will tell you what you are." What would he think of the fact that the first part of the formulation has become, more or less, a competitive sport, while the analysis never arrives, only the check?

My experience of contemporary food writing has been a great deal like my experience with sex writing. I've enjoyed it, I've taken part in it, I've read vast tracts of it. I still do. But the sheer volume, and the disparity of signal and noise, can easily burn me out.

When I am sickened by one too many extremophile excursions into offal-eating or Sardinian *casu marzu* (look it up), heartsick from yet more intensively over-romanticized fantasies of the "authentic" and "artisanal" and "rustic," bored witless by the gastronomic pissing contests of wannabe bad boys, and ready to gouge out my eyes if I am subjected to one more Instagrammed restaurant meal, I want to walk away forever. But I can't just walk away from eating. Or thinking about food, about what it means—and why it matters.

This is why I go back to M.F.K. Fisher. I read Fisher as a *digestif* and a corrective, as a reminder that it is possible to do better than the overindulgent and crazed. Fisher's careful prose reassures me that some people will always understand that things like food and drink have meaning and moment beyond the kitchen or market or mouth, that there are reasons to wait until after the thrilling instant has passed before you try to set such things down on the page. I go back to Fisher for these things because she helped me learn them in the first place.

I discovered Fisher when I was in the squalid blown flower of my late adolescence, and immediately became obsessive. I was not quite aware of just how callow I was then, but I suspected the worst. Fisher's books were talismans of a sophisticated, observant, elegant, artistic adulthood I desperately wanted, and her writing was, then as now, an antidote. It wasn't the excess of a boundlessly self-absorbed food culture that demanded her bracing, revivifying chaser then, though. Twenty-odd years ago, the thing I needed to be cured of was my own merciless, overblown self.

Unlike some Fisher fans, I was not particularly attracted to the specific circumstances of her life. Oh, I admired and aspired to her artistic success, her passionate loves, her independence, her worldliness. But I never envied her France and felt no romantic stirrings whatsoever at the images she painted of *vie bohème* grad-student poverty in shivering-cold apartments. I'd lived in Germany as a student already, and was a classical singer in training at a major conservatory, so all my friends were penniless musicians, poets, artists, and writers. That kind of poetry was practically the only thing I had in abundance.

What Fisher had that I so desperately wanted was style and self-assurance. Some of her sensual, unpretentious worldliness would've been nice, too. And I would've sold my soul for even a hint of the discernment. The dictum "less is more" had doubtless fallen upon my shell-like ears once or twice. I even recognized its value: I had, after all, managed to become a Fisher fan. But at the time I was about as capable of restraint and subtlety as I was capable of unassisted flight.

I was ashamed of my self-indulgent but helpless intensity. When I sang, I sang big and interpreted bigger. No high note went unswelled, no particularly poignant phrase unmilked. Had there been scenery in the practice rooms where I rehearsed arias and art songs, I would've chewed it like a teething Rottweiler. I poured out much too much, and I knew it. I felt it. I was informed of it repeatedly by voice teachers and diction coaches. But I could not seem to stop myself from doing it.

It was the same way when I wrote, and I did so a great deal. Melodrama and hyperbole gushed forth, yet I continually felt incapable and incompetent to express myself fully no matter how many fulminant intensifiers I brought to bear. This embarrassed me, but then again, so did just about everything I put to paper. Even as I was writing them down, the silliness and childishness, triteness and immaturity of my words made me writhe. Almost everyone is somewhat ridiculous at that age, and I knew it was normal, but I hated it nonetheless. If I knew better, why couldn't I do better?

From my earliest encounters with Fisher's work, I realized I was in the presence of someone who embodied as a writer the precise sorts of things I, as a classical singer, was expected to embody both onstage and off: she was feminine, cultured, intelligent, seductive, expressive, not just talented but also skilled. Fisher had, in other words, the entirety of the arsenal of the successful singer at her command, up to and including the canniness to know not just how to seduce, but *when*. Fisher confirmed what I already knew: that raw materials would never be enough. Everything hung on discernment and simplicity. It is no accident that the single best-known sentence of Fisher's sizable oeuvre consists of just five plain, unfussy words: "I was really very hungry." The sentence packs a great deal of nuance and subtext, of course, about Fisher's unapologetic carnality, about her appreciation of appetite, about her willingness to address her appetites on her own terms. But the sentence is direct and unqualified. It is one of the things that makes her writing so instantly, so readily identifiable as hers and no one else's. Consider sentences like these:

> There are several things to do with oysters beside eat them, although many people believe firmly in that as the most sensible course. ["Pearls Are Not Good To Eat," *Consider the Oyster*]

> Biddy breakfasted with Biddy, and saw in a mirror clearly, for the first of many times. ["On Dining Alone," *Serve it Forth*]

At the time, such straightforward, intelligent, declarative sentences were a somewhat atypical product for a feminine pen. Possibly this is the sturdy verbal inheritance of a newspaperman's daughter. Fisher grew up, in part, in the pressroom of her father's small-town southern California daily, and was in her teens one of the paper's regular stringers. After Fisher began to publish on her own, she noted with amusement and satisfaction that early readers could not tell that she was a woman. There is of course no reason clear-eyed straightforwardness cannot be a feminine characteristic. In person it often is. But when women write, especially about food or love, they are strongly encouraged to hew to a set of gendered expectations that include a certain level of sentimentality and frilliness. Their absence marks Fisher as an outlier.

It also makes her effective. It was from Fisher that I first learned the value of stating plainly what you want the reader to believe. Fisher does not hedge or qualify her statements. It seems always as if she is simply reporting. For a woman as careful and canny as Fisher, and as devoted to control of her divulgences, this is a brilliant tool. Fisher is not precisely duplicitous. But her writerly persona is created, in large part, by things she does not disclose.

What she offered publicly she offered deliberately. Her emotions—her recollections—are curated. As a historian I am particularly sensitive to this. Left to itself, the past is like fallen leaves, and either rots or gets scattered on the winds depending on where it lands. To become a story, let alone one that repays the telling or the reading, it needs insight, context, emotion. These must have their own internal logic. This ability to be able to limn something deftly and briefly, rather than with embarrassing effulgence, was a thing I desperately craved, as a young artist. Fisher's almost magical ability to deliver a punch without raising more than a finger was, and still is, remarkable.

His table manners were dreadful, and I resented him

even more than he did me, probably. ["The Measure of My Powers, 1930–1931, *The Gastronomical Me*]

Nobody but Aunt Gwen ever made fried egg sandwiches for us. Grandmother was carefully protected from the fact that we had ever even heard of them, and as for Mother, preoccupied with a second set of children, she shuddered at the thought of such grease-bound proteins with a thoroughness which should have made us chary but instead succeeded only in satisfying our human need for secrets. ["H is for Happy," *An Alphabet for Gourmets*]

From the perspective of my own queer, high femme sensibilities, though, I have never been able to see Fisher's discernment in a purely literary light. I have always viewed it as also being a mode of the femme tactic, applicable in seduction and all other instances of interpersonal warfare, of manufacturing surfaces that will generate the desired sorts of traction.

That Fisher leans toward the sensual is surely a matter of inclination as well as strategy. But the strategy is there too. She understood playing to one's audience. As she writes in *An Alphabet for Gourmets*, "the great courtesans have paid less attention to the Freudian appearance of their kitchens' masterpieces, from what I can gather, than to the temperaments of the men they have willed to please." Fisher's admissions of lust and hunger, the ways she wrote openly about seduction and love and her own — desires, were calculated to appeal most and best to the men to whom she is unapologetically, openly attracted. (They also appealed to women. This may or may not have been something Fisher would've wanted to think about, as I will discuss.) That this is a matter of femme discernment is apparent to me from the vigor and calm with which she talks about these things, as well as their frequency in her work. For a middle-class, straight, white woman of her generation, it was still a bit outré to admit casually to multiple marriages, an awareness of when one is being seduced, or an appreciation for "a bonny figure . . . tall, lean, and wholesome . . . physically at least. (Spiritually he is a disciple of Henry Miller, which in some people's eyes is a form of disease.)"

There is nothing furtive, accidental, apologetic, or ingenuous in Fisher's femme performance. I have long suspected that the lack of apology, in conjunction with her French expat's semi-foreignness, was part of what allowed her to get away with writing things as she did of a rural troublemaker and locally legendary *bon vivant*: "Cesar was all that every man wants secretly to be: strong, brave; foul, cruel, reckless; desired by women and potent as a goat; tender and very sweet with children; feared by the priest; respected by the mayor; utterly selfish and as generous as a prince; gay. Cesar was man. Man noble and monstrous again after so many centuries." But it was also partly because such enthusiastic connoisseurship of the male animal appealed to the male animal in her readers. What straight man, after all, could read such evocative writing and then resist seeing his own reflection when she went on to write something like "Given the fact that I have found a male of about my own age, healthy, not too nervous, fairly literate, in other words, one I would like to have cleave unto me for reasons of pleasure if not reproduction . . ."?

Fisher did not adore all men equally, to be sure, but she gave them her allegiance in a way she did not give to other women. Her cool collusions with the male gaze and her consistent habit of judging, criticizing, and dismissing other women have made her unpopular among some feminists. There are many, many examples of this in her work, but the ones that always come to mind for me are Fisher's unforgettable naming, in *Consider the Oyster*, of a "very very terrible very very divine woman of the upper classes" as "La Belle Dame sans Culottes," and her merciless depiction of one of her brother's girlfriends as "a very pretty pale limp one . . . [who] drooped everywhere, her eyelids, her little pink mouth, her slender shoulders . . . ," and whose effects on Fisher's brother were "ghastly."

But such skewering of other women is, in its self-promoting cruelty, also a classic act of femme discernment and strategy. Matter-of-factly dismantling other women, especially through backhanded compliments and damning with faint praise, is a traditional high femme trick, exposing the critical flaws of the competition where everyone can see it done. It has often seemed to me that the only females in Fisher's work who escape this are her beloved sister, Norah, and her two daughters, Anne and Kennedy. No coincidence, I think, that these were among the few women who could not possibly constitute any sort of competition. The rest are routinely undercut by practiced, typically understated swipes of Fisher's razor-sharp pen.

Tellingly, Fisher's classic alpha-femme approach to other women loses its edge when she is faced with female queerness. She is out of her element. Outrage and confusion overcome discernment and canniness, and Fisher becomes messy, scattered, and banal. In "The First Oyster," a story of a holiday party at the boarding school Fisher attended as a young woman, her descriptions of being the object of an older girl's ardor are queasy, frantic, and unsophisticated: ". . . she was the most horrible creature I had ever known. Perhaps I might kill her some day. I was going to be sick."

Much later, in the 1941 essay "Feminine Ending," Fisher wrote about a trip to Mexico, and the shock of discovering that a local mariachi singer in whom her brother was intensely invested was a woman living and performing as a man. Fisher arrogantly re-genders Juanito as "Juanita" and insists on using feminine pronouns for him, apparently as the only way that she is capable of comprehending the emotional tension she senses between her brother and the singer. Perhaps the risk of considering her brother capable of such intensity regarding another male was too much. Perhaps contemplating the queerness of—and the potential for her own erotic traction with—a man of female experience was unbearable. Somehow one would expect less of a kneejerk reaction from one so worldly, so self-assured, so certain of the directions of her own gendered desires. One would, in short, expect more discernment.

There are some other cracks in her straight-femme discernment. (Of course I looked for them.) In "The Lemming to the Sea," a 1938 tale of a friendship Fisher enters into with a man during an ocean-liner crossing of the Atlantic, in which Fisher takes the unusual and hardly credible approach of acting as if she has not registered the man's intense romantic and sexual interest in her until her husband's jealousy makes it obvious. Perhaps Fisher genuinely did employ the time-honored femme device of pointedly, publicly *not noticing* someone to whom she had no reciprocal attraction. It is, however, a tactic that can only be employed if one is first aware of the other person's interest. It seems illogical to me, aware as my reading has made me of Fisher's finely tuned heterosexual antennae, to think she was not.

Yet I can only speculate, because the way Fisher writes it actually works. She knows how to be the narrator but not the narrative even when the story is one of her own very personal experiences. It is sleight of hand as much as it is anything. By talking about other people rather than herself, describing their actions and reactions—which of course means describing what she perceives of them and interprets them to mean—Fisher displaces herself from the reader's awareness and simultaneously becomes their awareness quite entirely. It makes it difficult to argue with her. When Fisher, describing an odd and awkward visit by the man with whom she had her shipboard friendship, recounts that she and Parrish took "Jacques" to dinner ". . . and ate piles of perch filets on a big platter in the cafe," and continues "I don't think Jacques had ever eaten so simply that way, with a lady and gentleman in a common-man's place," we accept it, though how would we know? How would she? Every appearance of a person or a thing, every motive or reaction she ascribes to others is in reality Fisher's own. This knack for intimate-seeming observation without self-revelation or interiority is its own mode of discernment . . . and direction.

It took me many years of reading Fisher to see this. I felt stunned, and a little betrayed, the day I realized that Fisher, the great memoirist, was actually an intensely private person whose narratives of her own experience throughout her many books showed only that which she wished the reader to see. Surely this came as such a shock in part because I was so very sloppy and unrefined, my boundaries so porous. But probably it was also because it was a time where, everywhere I turned, deliberate and sometimes egregious subjectivity was becoming increasingly prized. In life as well as in literature, emotion and subjective response were gaining a new, strangely hypnotic power. This was the early 1990s, the era where it became common and acceptable for a student to answer a professor's question with "I feel like . . ." instead of "I think." Soon it would be *comme il faut* even for newscasters.

Now, in spite of my long history of ambivalence and shame about my own feelings, I have a deep and serious respect for emotion in general, and for the truths emotions may reveal that mere fact cannot. I also have grave reservations about treating emotion as if it were the whole of the facts. There is value in combing emotions and facts together between reason's carding-paddles before they are spun into yarn.

Or into *a* yarn. Fisher is a virtuoso at this, which is one of the reasons that her direction—or misdirection, if you prefer—can be so hard to see. Into this mix, Fisher twines two more of her remarkable skills, two more things that the youthful me (to say nothing of the current version) would've liked very much to know how to do as well. In Fisher, seduction and the expression of opinion go hand in hand. They are synergistic.

Here is the single most practical thing I ever learned from M.F.K. Fisher: seduction is not the art of showing someone that you want them. That is merely a proposition, no matter how artfully it is done. Seduction, properly done, is the art of inducing a desirable second party to want *you* to want *them*. The reflection of desire is critical. Without that mutuality, seduction is just pursuit on one side and capitulation on the other, and frankly less fun than it seems like it should be, particularly when the game is no longer new.

Fisher alludes to seductions in various bits of her oeuvre, both her own and other people's, as often with the sharpness of her femme perspicacity as with fondness or excitement. As for the real seductions in Fisher's work, they involve the author, and are thus more impressions than demonstrations. She never divulged too much about her own personal amorous doings. But there are a few scenes in which we see Fisher seduced or seducing, in earnest. One of the most fully written of these details a secret Easter midnight supper of caviar served by her beloved Dillwyn Parrish in Parrish's candle-lit, flower-bedecked studio in their shared home in Switzerland. It ends not with Fisher and Parrish tumbling into bed but with Fisher thanking him and shyly, primly walking to her own room. Yet there is no mistaking what is going on: Fisher writes that having found a hand-illustrated invitation on her desk, she made herself "look as beautiful as I could," then ascended the stairs to the studio with a small gift. The effort is mutual. Parrish has gone out of his way to make the room and himself desirable to Fisher, including setting forth a large tin of caviar and a bottle of excellent gin, two of her favorite treats. That "every swallow of the liquor was as hot and soft as the candle flames around us," and they "talked, more and better than we ever talked with anyone else," comes as no surprise. It is fabulous, cinematic, achingly desirable, and it is both circumspect and discreet, a triumph of selective self-presentation.

It is in such acts of creating the self that will make the Other wish she would want him, that we find the foundation of Fisher's work and perhaps of her person. This is precisely where opinion enters into it.

Even when we do not necessarily share the sentiments we tend to admire firm and unfragile opinions tempered with intellect and erudition as well as experience. It is, we know, easier to go through life without such things. Many of us have been scolded or intimidated out of some of ours. We look up to those who express strong opinion graciously, without silencing or condescending. We respect such people, and we want their respect in turn—and their good opinion. We want them to like us, to find us worthwhile, to have a good opinion of us on the same sturdy, articulate footing.

Sometimes we fight back against our wanting to be wanted, our preference for being preferred. It does make us vulnerable, and vulnerability can breed resentment. Some readers react angrily to Fisher's opinionatedness, calling her arrogant and smug. I have occasionally felt that way myself. When I first fell in love with her, though, I just wanted to be, to embody, the sort of thing she might like. I was tremblingly seducible . . . and it made me tremendously teachable.

What did my love teach me? If nothing else, Fisher taught me the valuable skill of detecting a crucial sort of category error, the confusion of form and substance. Good food, as Fisher resolutely and repeatedly reminds the reader, has nothing to do with *haute cuisine*. Fisher's work participates in a metanarrative that has become a cliché of the food-writing genre, the one a clear-sighted friend once referred to as "*Pilgrim's Progress* to Paris" in which the American of (of course) stunted and parochial palate goes to France and experiences culinary enlightenment. But it is also true that this was in Fisher's case, happenstance.

Fisher herself does not put her cart before that horse. She does not buy into the notion that "exquisite" or "ostentatious" are synonymous with quality or pleasure, nor does

she err in believing it of "rustic" or "artisanal" or "peasant."
All these things are found in both good and bad versions in
Fisher's tales. Indeed, Fisher embraces even bad food, when
it has integrity in her eyes. She discerns what is important
to her about a meal or a dish, and having done so, says what
it is. Her concatenation of thought and emotion is what
seduces. Our agreement or disagreement is of no moment.
A successful seduction, as Fisher made clear, need not end
with things going bump in the night.

I am now not as easily seduced by Fisher, unless I want
to be. When I go back to Fisher now it is not with my old
desire to be caught in her discerning web. For one thing I
can see its strands now, and can even pull off some of the
same tricks myself, though I make no pretenses to doing
it as well. Still I enjoy and admire her sturdy, uncompli-
cated language, the sense of the anchoring animal self-fil-
tered through an intelligent, selective mind, the thoughtful
worldliness, the various modes of discernment that make her
words a real communication, however directive, and not just
another reflexive immature yawp. (Oh, the Internet has a lot
to answer for!) These are the things that made me cling so
hungrily to Fisher in the first place, and they are what bring
me back to Fisher now.

Voluptuousness need not mean excessiveness, Fisher
taught me that. Calm assertion is nine tenths of authority.
Emotion is more potent without melodrama, or even excla-
mation points. She taught me that too. Discernment is the
result of having something specific to say. The sturdiness

of an opinion is directly correlated to the degree to which it stands on its own. The seductiveness of an opinion is directly correlated to the degree to which its holder stands on *her* own. All were good and needed lessons.

They were good books, too, prose and ideas strong enough to weather all the fulminant emotion and ambivalence and angst I had within. That Fisher has with time—and the unasked-for bounty of the current foodie explosion—become my chosen antidote to the outside world's excessiveness is only to be expected. I read her because it works.

So when from time to time I become badly bloated, as I do, with the hysterical and greedy and caricatured and contrived of the foodie universe, I simply go back to where I started. I do not visit the food blogs, I shun the magazines, I avoid at all costs the accidental viewing of food-related television, I do not go to restaurants. I eat scrambled eggs on hot, well-browned, Marmite-smeared toast. I drink tea, and water, both with lemon, and sometimes bourbon or brown ale without. I steam fish, or cube fresh tofu, and dress them with soy sauce and sesame oil and a dab of chili paste. A not insignificant quantity of popcorn, popped in olive oil and well-salted, occurs, sometimes for supper. Onions, cucumbers, cabbage, chard. Apples in season, or peaches, or grapefruit, once in a while lychees. If I feel I can handle something so decadent, I may eat a steak, salted and seared in a pan hot enough to put a seductive crust on the outside without taking the inside past a firm bright red, and chase it with a good bitter beer. (Fisher would approve at least of this.) There is fairly little real cookery involved, but that's a different thing entirely. There is substance, and worthy things that are good to eat. And alongside them, lying open on the table as I eat, there is often a volume of M.F.K. Fisher, still and again, bearing witness to whatever small scraps I may have acquired of discernment and simplicity and the calm fortitude to eat and drink as it pleases me.

II

Nothing about it was okay, and nothing about it would ever be okay again. I had just seen my first portrait photograph of Mary Frances Kennedy Fisher, one of those from her youth in which she is elegant, dewy, and luminous, and it had confirmed my awkward, nameless despair.

Fisher was beautiful, remarkably so. She was beautiful as I was not, am not, and will never be. Soigné, creamy, lanky.

It would be dishonest to say that I felt betrayed. No lumpy, dark, hairy, fat, Midwestern girl reaches early adulthood still in the possession of the ability to feel betrayed, or surprised in any way at all, that the world loves the long-legged, savannah-ready blonde of California in ways it will never love the squishy, pale Slavs of Cleveland. But suddenly there she was, gazing calmly, coolly, gorgeously out from a book jacket, and I would never be able to read her words the same way again.

My love for M.F.K. Fisher blossomed in my early undergraduate years, courtesy of the peerless generosity of the Boston Public Library. Like all late adolescents and early twentysomethings, I wanted things. I wanted to be taken seriously, I wanted to be loved, I wanted to be desired, I wanted to excel and impress. I wanted experiences and intensity but also refinement and subtlety. Most of all I wanted to be able to do anything, anything at all, half so beautifully and well as Fisher could love and travel and eat and move through the world and write about it all.

My very first taste of Fisher was one of her many cookbook forewords, the preface to the first edition of Shizuo Tsuji's groundbreaking 1980 *Japanese Cooking: A Simple Art*. My mother had given me the book as a backhanded gift, having decided, in a fit of magical thinking, that the cookery of the enviably slim Japanese would make her fat daughter slender too, with no idea that she was giving me an unusually excellent cookbook, or an iconic writer whose work would change who I was.

I mention it because neither that cookbook, nor the first half-dozen or so Fisher titles I subsequently devoured, featured either Fisher's likeness or any physical description of her. This seems strange now, when it's hard to buy one of Fisher's books without getting a picture-show into the bargain. But I encountered Fisher before the point in the early 1990s when the facial preoccupations of film and television started to become integral to the publishing industry. Earlier editions of Fisher's books are photograph-free. There are little "About the Author" notes, but sometimes not even that. My 1978 reprint of her 1949 translation of Brillat-Sa-varin—which is much more an edition than a translation, laced liberally with the distinctive flavor of Fisher's own insights—bears not a single sentence about M.F.K. herself, let alone a photograph. By contrast, I do not own a single volume of Fisher's work published after 1988 that does not somewhere bear her now-iconic likeness.

For some years I thought it ironic that the implacably sensory Fisher entered my awareness in such a disembodied way. In rereading great chunks of long-neglected Fisher as I prepared to work on this project, though, I realized that no, it is not ironic: it is probably what she would've preferred.

Fisher, as she styles herself particularly in *Two Towns in Provence*, is a ghost. A professional one. She seems a memoirist at heart, and perhaps she was. Much of her writing is at the intersection of intimate observation and personal reflection, but Fisher seems to me to be a character in her narratives only rarely. She is even more rarely an actor, despite the sometimes lavish amounts of activity she records. She observes, she witnesses, she imagines, she reflects, reminisces, and reports. Indeed she acts and reacts, but she often seems strangely devoid of articulated initiatives, motives, and desires of her own.

So infrequently is Fisher a present player on her own stage—and let me just point out how very, how vastly far away this is from the currently fashionable soiled-kitchen-whites chest beating and home-cook's confessionals that occupy so much of the food writing shelves—that I recall many of those moments in detail far disproportionate to the length of the passages themselves. Her famous description of preparing peas at Le Pâquis is part of a tender vivid evocation of a lost world of Swiss meadows and doomed love. But it is as memorable for the fact that it shows us Fisher *actually cooking*, in the present tense, an activity startlingly infrequent in her work.

Then there is the throwaway final paragraph of "B is for Bachelors" (*An Alphabet for Gourmets*, 1949) in which Fisher states ". . . the main mistake was in his trying to entertain a woman in that condition as if she were still seducible and / or he still a bachelor: we had already been married several months." A beautiful comic turn, but it works because it is a rare moment in which she gives the reader her own self in the awkward medias res of real, uncurated life.

She shows the reader precisely, and only, what she wishes them to see. There is an arrogance to it that I appreciate even when I do not like it. But I couldn't see it until after I'd seen her face.

I was blind to Fisher's careful self-presentation because I was blind to her as a human being. Fisher's ghostliness made my readerly transference easy, almost insidiously so. With the qualities that made her no doubt as *insolite*, as singular and characteristic as the Marseilles she adored, left mostly unarticulated, it was possible to imagine that in whatever particulars she did not describe of herself Fisher was, in fact, like me.

I do not believe that I am the only person to have had

this experience of Fisher. On the contrary, I strongly suspect that her ability to sublimate Mary Frances whilst still offering her eyes, her mouth, her hands, her vocabulary for the vicarious experience of the reader is the secret of her continued success. It was certainly the soil in which my own adoration rooted. So long as I could imagine that Fisher was much like me, I could also imagine that I was much like Fisher. This in turn afforded me the luxury of fancying that I too might be the kind of person who could write with such pleasing, intelligent strength, such beautiful, clear simplicity. At nineteen I craved few things more. If I'm honest, the idea still holds charm, even though I now have a much better idea of just how much squalor and pain Fisher hid in her vaporous realm of ghosts.

Then I saw my first photograph of Fisher. I had not expected the crack it made in the foundations of my love for her, or the way that crack widened to allow a flood of other, increasingly complicated, observations.

Post-photo, I read Fisher more carefully, searching for signs of the body and the face I had seen in the picture. They were few. There were some occasional passing remarks about trying to look beautiful for a lover or a special event, or feeling out of place being too brown and thin for a formal dinner. (That it is virtually impossible to imagine someone today complaining of feeling too tan and too thin for a fancy evening out is another of those things that anchors Fisher's work securely in another era.) But in her published work, at least, it seemed to me as if Fisher's body and appearance were of very little moment to her. It is unlikely that she would not have known she was beautiful. I presumed at the time that she likely took her beauty—as have so many of the effortlessly beautiful girls I have known—as simply her birthright, which of course it is. Beautiful or unbeautiful, the bodies and the faces that we are born with are just the ones we have. They become so boringly familiar that we hardly see them any more unless for some reason our reflections, or a photograph, provide an angle that takes us by surprise.

There is nothing fair or unfair about natural beauty. Like other innate physical traits—a pleasing voice, an extraordinary sense of balance—it is evidence of nothing but the luck of the draw. I have always been aware of this, as a classical singer with a voice I have been told since early childhood was a "gift from God." My peculiar vocal beauty was not an internal but audible sign of grace; it was merely a fluke. I knew that anyone else's organically beautiful face or form was not so different.

But outward beauty works differently from other forms of glorious bodily happenstance. There is a great deal that is fair and unfair about that.

There is a price a woman has to be able to pay, a bar she must be able to reach, if she is to be allowed to desire and enjoy the world rather than be expected merely to serve it. Every unbeautiful woman knows coldly and exactly what the one currency is that is universally accepted for that transaction, because she has learned that she does not possess it. For us, the unlovely, the ungraceful, the unslender, permission to enjoy the world lies up a steep, rocky hill, one on which we are likely to stumble in full view of those already enjoying the view from the top. And we know it.

So long as I was ignorant of the embodied Fisher, and so long as I could still imagine her intelligence, perception, taste, and talent were at the center of it all, I could imagine that perhaps I might manage to do as well on the same basis. This was an encouraging thought and it lasted precisely as long as I did not know that Mrs. Fisher was beautiful. Once I did, I began to find it hard to trust the easy voluptuary nature of Fisher's prose, which I had previously found satisfyingly indulgent. It became difficult to tolerate the catlike, inward-looking expressions of pleasure in sex and food and travel I had formerly enjoyed and wanted to share. Fisher, it seemed to me, owed her access to these things and her ability to claim them so publicly not mostly to brains or boldness, as I had imagined, but to beauty.

At that age I did not yet have a vocabulary to express the inequities of privilege, no way to begin to make sense of the deep and systematic prejudices we hold about beauty and bodies. But when I saw her photo I knew instantly that the life Fisher led was closed to me, and it was closed for reasons far more personal and material than the fact that I would never live in Dijon in the 1920s or Aix in the 1950s. Unlike Fisher, my body, my face would never offer me the kind of privilege hers provided to her. Specifically, my body and face would never allow me the incomparable privilege of not much noticing that I had them.

It is of course possible that Fisher was entirely aware of her physical grace, beauty, and the privilege that devolved upon her as a result. Perhaps she felt that such things were, like the day-to-day details of her daughters, divorces, or dish-washing, too vulgar or perhaps tedious to mention. I simply don't know. What I do know is that I still have the sense, unsupportable in any concrete way, that to Fisher her body was mostly neutral. Perhaps sometimes she felt it was a valuable asset, or knew that it was. But when her body exists in her writing it is mostly present without comment, just an animal vehicle through which she engaged with and enjoyed the world.

I could not, and still cannot, quite imagine what this must be like.

Then and now, I could imagine what it might be like to have one's appearance be an asset. Like virtually every other girl I knew who was not conventionally pretty or beautiful, I had fantasized about what it would be like to have looks that opened doors for you. This was not a matter of being sexually desired—even at twenty I understood full well that beauty and fuckability were not the same thing. All my life I had witnessed prettier girls, and often merely slenderer girls, getting better service in shops and restaurants, getting only warnings in situations where other people got traffic tickets, getting chosen in auditions where I and other less lovely women had given better musical and vocal performances, and so on.

Though its exchange rate be ever so inconstant, beauty

is nevertheless a form of capital. But it is a strange one. It cannot change hands, and is rarely openly acknowledged by either side as a bargaining chip. To do so would change the nature of the transaction, show your hand, betray the ways the deck is stacked. It is safer to do what we traditionally do, and pretend the beauty is of no consequence, nothing but neutral.

In some ways, this is even true: the so-called "good" bodies and beautiful faces of our culture are neutral in that they simply don't get singled out for abuse. But this in itself is a form of privilege. I must note here that experience of one's body as neutral, not a target of any sort, is distinctly a more masculine experience of the body than it is a feminine one. Just moving through the world in a female body can be enough to get you singled out for trouble. Moving through the world unremarked, unbothered, experiencing your own self in the world as "normal" is not the simple thing we convince ourselves it is. It is definitely not neutral. But it easily passes for it. It is a game changer, whether the beautiful person experiences it as one or not.

But such theory came later. In the moment that I saw her photo, all I knew was that Fisher was beautiful. What I knew from her books is that as far as she was concerned her body was a neutral thing, unexceptional and left largely undescribed. In other words, no, she was not like me at all.

Once I noticed how absent Fisher's body was from her writing, how apparently little it factored into her experience of her day-to-day, I realized just how horridly, insistently present my body was in my own. When I tried to mentally insert my actual body, rather than Fisher's so-neutral-as-to-be-absent one, into Fisher's scenes, I realized with a sudden humiliated flush just how very much wish-fulfillment I had been vicariously deriving from Fisher's nonchalant physical neutrality.

For the entirety of my conscious life my body has been various sizes of fat, and as such inconvenient, unlovely, and often unaccommodated. I am obligated to assess on a daily basis things like the irritation of fellow users of public transit who discover they must share a bench seat with a fat girl; the likelihood that any given clothes shop will have anything in my size that is not a scarf or handbag; whether a cafe chair will wobble under me or its arms gouge my hips; and whether any given passerby on the street will decide to verbally assault me for what is, in essence, my failure to be less physically remarkable. Things Fisher writes neutrally of doing, like taking a seat at a sidewalk cafe or just going for a walk, I have never done without performing a complex calculus with multiple variables, including whether I am psychically equipped to cope with it if things go wrong. A fat woman's body may be many things. It may be a spectacle. It may be a bad example. It may be tolerated, though it is more likely to be despised. What it is not is neutral.

Little wonder I was so easily enthralled by Fisher's combination of physical neutrality and sensory pleasure. Little wonder that I felt betrayed when I realized Fisher's neutrality of embodiment was the wake that trailed behind her physical privilege. Little wonder that I began to resent Fisher's ability to do the two things for which she is most and most justly celebrated, namely, eat and drink.

I turned my back on Fisher for a bit. Fisher's was not the only possible model on which a woman might have come to enjoy a career of travel and gastronomy in the early years of the American twentieth century, and I knew it. An unlovely girl might also eat and drink and write intelligently and professionally, if she were sufficiently dynamic, hardworking, and well-connected, or so the *New York Herald Tribune*'s legendary Clementine Paddleford's example testified. Today Paddleford is all but forgotten. Nevertheless, in her brisk, workaday way she ruled the newspaper food-writing roost around the same time as Fisher was earning the sobriquet "the poet of the appetites."

A plain, raw-boned woman from Kansas, Paddleford's genius lay in showcasing the skills of farm wives, household servants, and chefs from New York and New Orleans with equal enthusiasm and care. In an era when few newspaper food writers traveled much further than to judge the state fair pie contest, Paddleford logged more than 50,000 miles yearly in her efforts to chronicle how America cooked and ate.

Fisher's writing career, on the other hand, was something of an accident that arose initially from the circumstances of having followed her first husband to Dijon when he went there to study. Her later career took a motley collection of writerly turns reflecting the vagaries of marriages, illnesses, children, and other personal vicissitudes, but her canon hardly shows it. I have often had the sense that there is a sort of silent conspiracy among Fisher fans that would have the world believe that the beautiful, exotic, and sophisticated (French!) Mrs. Fisher wrote only beautiful, exotic, sophisticated things, as though those were the only kind of eggs such a rara avis could possibly lay. (How these people rationalize *How to Cook a Wolf*, or Fisher's recollections of her grandmother's despotic digestion, I have never been quite sure.)

It also often feels as if there is an additional conspiracy around Fisher, one in which she herself participated to some degree through her artful elisions, to portray Fisher as a lily of the field, who was beautiful and did not labor (although she certainly did), and definitely not as someone who "had a job." Paddleford, by contrast, resolutely American and with a face made for radio, was a professional who strongly identified with the hardworking and commonplace. The beautiful, quasi-foreign evocative poet of the appetites beloved of Updike and Auden; the homely hometown girl with a great personality, bosom buddies with Duncan Hines.

There was however, one physical trait, and one social privilege, that Paddleford and Fisher shared. They were both built long-limbed and lean. Fisher was beautiful enough that she could afford to be seen feeding herself. Paddleford did not have enough physical charm that enthusiastic eating would have been thought to detract from it. Neither was fat. Culturally speaking, each woman had as much permission to eat as any woman was going to get, and each, in her way, ran with it.

It is necessary, I think, to insert a word here about the rebellion and self-assertion it requires for women to eat, particularly in public and for pleasure. Much is made, these days, about the effects of a genuinely fascist body culture that sets zero—literal nothingness—as the optimal dress size, and in which no woman's body, be it ever so thin, is ever "good" enough for long. This has not always existed in quite so severe a form. During Fisher and Paddleford's heyday, a girl could indeed still be too thin, if not too rich. Fatness was, to be sure, not a desirable characteristic, but the range of "acceptable" feminine sizes was wider and the pervasive mythos that a "good body" is possible if only a woman does all the right things in all the right ways was not yet the cultural lodestone it is now.

It is arguably more difficult for women to eat by their own rights now than it was when Fisher and Paddleford were at their peak. Yet even then, women did not have carte blanche when it came to feeding themselves. There were appropriately feminine ways to eat. Women were, as they still are, expected to take an interest in food that was essentially focused on others, particularly husbands and children. It's more important that they know how to cook for others than that they know how they like to feed themselves.

Women were also, as they still are, expected to limit their eating in the interest of maintaining their image. Women have for centuries been counseled to eat little and lightly in front of other people if they would be seen to be attractive, delicate, and discreet. Salads, not steaks. Sweets, not Scotch. The supposedly irresistible allure of chocolate, even if one would really prefer a glass of port and a tart apple. One way or another, what and how women are supposed to eat has a great deal to do with satisfying other people, and only coincidentally themselves.

Eating to satisfy one's self, by contrast, is mostly a male prerogative. Men have permission—from their culture if not their cardiologists—to eat what they enjoy and to eat as much of it as they like. Gluttony can be macho (see also *Man v. Food*, and the entirety of the Anthony Bourdain/David Chang/Andrew Zimmern spectrum). And men, unlike women, have blanket permission to consume food without being involved in producing it. This means a lot: being cooked for, shopped for, having your menus planned for you, not having to concern yourself much with the tastes or dietary needs of others. If that weren't enough, it also means being entitled to pass judgment on whatever you happen to eat.

Personally and professionally, Fisher and Paddleford ate like men. They ate a great deal of food prepared by others, and they thought about it, had opinions about it, educated themselves about it, wrote about it, talked about it. Fisher knew she ate like a man and acknowledged it, even writing about it and the reactions it could provoke—with understanding but not empathy—in the 1938 piece "The Lemming to the Sea."

Both women were good cooks when they had a mind to be. Neither, it appears, was particularly devoted to it. Paddleford turned over all recipe-testing duties to the *Tribune*'s test kitchen staff, while Fisher, arguably the foremother of American food writing, rarely appears as a cook in her own food narratives. Some of Fisher's most startling revelations, to me, are the moments when she let slip that she at least sometimes existed in a traditionally feminine culinary mold, cooking for and serving food to others. The image of her preparing and serving *How to Cook a Wolf*'s parenthetical buttermilk-and-shrimp soup to "unconscious but happy hordes" was so surprising to me when I first read the book that I prepared the soup for myself almost immediately in my college dorm room, one of the three recipes from her books I have ever essayed. Later references to hired cooks seemed somehow more in character for her, as indeed do all her descriptions of eating at landladies' tables, in restaurants, and in the homes of friends.

What Fisher and Paddleford ate also bucked convention. There were, inevitably, appropriately feminine, light dishes like omelets and sweets, salads and consommés. But there was also unapologetic carnality. Paddleford talks about platters full of barbecue, whole lobsters, endless rows of planked shad. Fisher speaks of well-hung game, and wrote an entire slim book (a lover's gift to Dillwyn Parrish, the great love of her life) on oysters, which she loved best raw. Fisher also became an expert and erudite drinker, not only a masculine habit but a decidedly Continental, suspect one in post-Prohibition America.

Fisher and Paddleford were permitted to do these things partly because they had the chutzpah to do them. Fisher also had the privilege of beauty on her side, and the benefit of taking part (on whatever accidental basis) in a food culture not her own. Paddleford had homegrown plainness and the excuse of journalism. But it was still true then, as it is true now, that slender women may eat publicly in a way fat women may not.

We do not, by and large, trust fat women when it comes to eating. Beyond the superficial fear that they'll simply eat everything in their paths, we fear that they will eat indiscriminately. Fat women are excessive eaters, the supposed logic runs, probably also emotional ones who numb themselves with food the way alcoholics do with drink. They are unlikely, we think, to be judicious eaters, or sensitive ones, or ones who care about quality. Were they judicious eaters, eaters who chose quality over quantity, who ate only the best, and therefore were capable of trustworthy judgment in regard to food, they would not be fat, QED.

There are chubby women celebrity cooks now, Ina Garten and the like. But note that they are cooks, not eaters, and they are not really writers, certainly not in the way Fisher was. Their engagement with food is governed by feminine food rules. They cook to please, to teach others to please. Garten is fatter and older than the voluptuous, sensuously radiant Nigella Lawson, another supremely feminine and not thin (if also not precisely fat) cook-eater. So where Lawson is the sexy rich-man's-wife "nonchalantly" licking crème anglaise off her finger as she serves dessert at a posh party for her husband's colleagues, Garten is motherly, even grandmotherly, eminently approachable, reassuring, domestic, down-home, comforting.

But these women are not poets of the appetites, conjuring nuanced longings. They do not tempt readers to imagine the strange and wonderful pleasures beneath the "mildewed fat" insulating well-aged terrines, or in the tangled bowls of wild herbs and eggs stolen by night and served up by a locally famous eccentric. Nor are they indefatigable, encyclopedically knowledgeable, insatiably curious documentarians. Say what you will about Garten's co-opting of the "barefoot contessa" title, but she's old enough to know that it comes from a movie about what happens to women who refuse to take their proper role as dutiful wives and mothers, namely that they get shot. Garten's "contessa" is barefoot . . . and in the kitchen, preparing food for others, exactly where she should be.

Fat plus food equals woman, not man. Not even "like a man." We give that privilege grudgingly. My body has never earned me that privilege. Whatever glee, enthusiasm, knowledge, or discernment I may bring to the supper table has always been tempered by the knowledge that the world disapproves on general principles of my eating anything at all. The day I first saw a photograph of M.F.K. Fisher was the day I realized that while I hoped for the contrary, the world was unlikely to make any exceptions for me in that regard.

There is something true and right about the pain of a collapsing illusion. In the wake of losing my imaginary older-better-more-sophisticated-beautiful-slender-maybe-someday me, the dull truths of my own particular embodiment became easier to accept. It was not okay that Fisher's looks and her body earned her privilege and pleasure in ways mine would not, but it nevertheless was. As the knowledge sank in, I found I had less desire to pretend that things were otherwise, but also less desire to go along quietly with the notion that such unfairness was somehow legitimate and right just because it was real. My appetites were no less genuine. There was no particularly good reason that they ought not be as legitimate.

Many years later, as a sideways nod to Fisher, I gave a book of my erotica the title *Unruly Appetites*. I think she would've understood my choice, as a writer, to use the focusing lens of sex to write in and on the intersections of bodies and culture. It is, ultimately, what she herself quite consciously did with food, a thing that dawned on me not long after that first terrible, wonderful glimpse of the beautiful Mrs. Fisher. When I was forced to stop projecting myself into the blank spaces in Fisher's narratives, I had to begin again, and engage with what she actually did and said.

My love affair with Fisher's work was the last time I read as a child, and the first time I truly read as an adult. The headlong overidentification of my early days with Fisher is something I now recognize as the distinctive experience of reading as a child. Then a photograph made it impossible for me to pretend any longer that I read from within the words, actually experiencing them. Losing that was a deep, real loss. But learning to read as my own self, separate and sovereign, was a gift.

No, Fisher was not like me. None of the writers I love are. They see and notice and understand only what they see and write and understand with their own bodies, their own eyes and mouths and hearts, not what I would. That it is the reason writing matters, the reason reading matters. These acts of thinking and feeling and writing are all we have. We toss them into the gap between ourselves and others not as prescriptions or scriptures, not even because we have any certainty that they'll reach the other side. We do it because need and pleasure and hunger are difficult and necessary and inevitable and human, because they are our lot, because they are what we have. If we are lucky, as writers, our crooked, ink-stained fingers do come to caress other faces, and we never know it. Those faces are not ours. They are nothing like ours. That is the point.

HANNE BLANK is a writer and historian who has also worked in a variety of kitchens, including her own as a pop-up restaurateur. She is the author of numerous books including *Virgin: The Untouched History*, *Straight: The Surprisingly Short History of Heterosexuality*, and *A Girl's Gotta Eat*. She lives in Atlanta, Georgia, where she is affiliated with Emory University.

DANIELLE HENDERSON

on

BELL HOOKS

Maybe Mrs. Dieder did not think I could read. A worn rectangle of beige carpet marked out the parameters of our reading circle. We sat on the floor in the dull winter light of her second grade classroom, textbooks heavy in our laps, waiting for Neil Machever to pronounce the words on the page so that Erin Troncati, cross-legged next to him and furiously chewing the ends of her blond hair, could read the next sentence. The class displayed their agitation with bouncing knees and rolling eyes as Neil pulled his eyebrows close together and frowned. With the spark of impatience that even today prompts me to sigh loudly (when someone takes too long to put their groceries on the rubberized belt or holds up the movie ticket line when they refuse to put down their cell phone), I hung my head and in a low but audible voice mumbled, "Puerto Rico."

Mrs. Dieder, sitting in a chair that may as well have been a throne, turned her round face toward me, pushed her gold wire glasses higher up on her nose, and said, "Pardon me, Ms. Henderson? Did you have something to say?" Her gray curls shook around her face. Red splotches traveled up her neck. I was surprised to hear my name come out of her face. She had never called on me to read.

"PUERTO RICO," I said loudly, pronouncing it "poo-

AIR-tow REE-coh" with the same accent I had heard on a commercial when I watched TV after school. Didn't Neil watch TV? Didn't his mom sit with him at night and look at the brightly colored countries on the globe, or read him books about kids who did not live in Greenwood Lake, New York?

Mrs. Dieder turned her lips into a straight line tight against her teeth and waited a moment before lifting her eyebrows, saying, "Yes, that is how you pronounce it. Erin, continue." I was full of the pride of accomplishment even if it was not reflected in the faces around me. My classmates kept their heads down but raised their angry eyes in my direction, scowling at me for breaking the cardinal sin: do not make the most popular boy in class feel stupid, especially if you are black and a girl.

That I was black was more important to my classmates than any other fact of my life. No one cared that I loved playing on the swings at recess, or that I memorized all the words to the Vincent Price part of "Thriller." I got pretty good air when I jumped from the monkey bars, even if landing on the concrete underneath sometimes hurt my hands as I touched down, and I could braid my Barbie's hair really good. I could have shown them my collection of Garbage Pail Kids cards, and I would have shared the handful of five cent Hubba Bubba pieces I was allowed to pick out at Hanley's corner store on Saturdays if they let me.

"Nigger," they said. "My mom says you're a nigger."

"Why is your hair like that?"

"My dad says black people come from Africa. Are you from Africa?"

They did their best to remind me that I was a square peg in a round hole, as if they could bully the blackness out of me. No one thought to stop them, not even our teacher.

To call the place where I grew up "predominantly white" is an understatement. My family settled there when my New York City–born grandparents, eager to leave the political turmoil of 1960s Harlem, found a sleepy town where they thought they could raise their kids. Since my mom went to school there from the time she was nine years old, she knew firsthand the racial hostility I would face when she enrolled me in kindergarten a year early, but she was a single mother unable to keep up with my growing curiosity about the world. Not much had changed in the twenty years since she attended middle school. The world may have started to accommodate diversity, but the people of our sleepy town did not.

I learned about race from the outside in, caught in the crosshairs of intolerant, sheltered people, unable to understand why my skin color precluded me from having teachers pay attention to me in class, from making friends, or from having the same hopes for my life that other children had. I didn't have the language to explain how these childhood experiences shaped my life until half of it was over and I'd already moved far away from Greenwood Lake. I didn't understand how my own story fit into a larger cultural experience until I read bell hooks.

bell hooks was inaccessible to me in a school system that excluded women and minorities from its history lessons, but I found her when I went to college in 2006 at the age of thirty. A cultural critic, writer, and academic feminist who writes in an approachable, nonacademic way, hooks changed the landscape of feminism when she wrote *Feminist Theory: From Margin to Center*, a book that moved the discussion from empowerment for middle-class white women toward a more inclusive feminism by criticizing the feminist movement for routinely excluding minority voices. She wrote that book when she was still in college and published it in 1984, the same year my classmates were calling me a "nigger."

Obviously I would not have been able to understand her work in 1984. But when I read the first chapter of *Feminist Theory: From Margin to Center* I felt like she'd been waiting out there, to help me make sense of my life. Understanding her was crucial to reigniting my feminist identity; finding her at all was a miracle.

Ironically, we read hooks last in my women's studies class, after the instructor taught us about the legions of historically important white feminists. hooks's take on liberal individualism and the "one-dimensional perspective on women's reality" finally put words in the way of my feelings about belonging to a group that didn't seem to want me as a member:

Like Friedan before them, white women who dominate feminist discourse today rarely question whether or not their perspective on women's reality is true to the lived experiences of women as a collective group.

hooks wasn't condemning whiteness, but using her own life as a way to shine a light on the importance of what it means to claim feminism for women who can't access it in the same way.

It wasn't until I read bell hooks that I finally learned how to disconnect from the shame I felt about growing up poor. hooks was adept at writing her own life story, her travels from Kentucky kid to professor, tying together her history with that of the larger black cultural history all along the way. My grandparents taught me about the civil rights movement so I thought I knew what it meant to be black. But through hooks, instead of seeing blackness as something that hindered me, I finally learned how my own story fit into the larger cultural context of displacement.

My awkwardness as one of a handful of minority students in a mostly white town wasn't helped by my strange family structure. My mother, who is alive and well, didn't raise me; I was raised instead by my grandparents. My mother abandoned my older brother and me to live with her drug-addict boyfriend, but not before we lived with them for three years. My mother was not a drug user but she was codependent, and believed she had the power to change people with love.

I've never met my father. When she ran away with him after high school she felt that he could be changed with love, that he would stop sleeping with other women and finally settle down with her. He left before I was born.

In the early years, my mother worked hard to support my brother and me. She had a full-time job soldering computer components onto tiny green plastic boards, and often picked up shifts at a restaurant. Welfare and food stamps helped her feed us. In the summer we played outside all day while my mom was at work. After dinner, we stayed outside and played until the streetlights came on; if we were thirsty, we drank from the hose on the side of Maureen Lafferty's house, and if we were hot, we found a leafy tree to run circles around in the shade. My brother and I were mostly on our own.

My friends lived in houses, but we had an apartment over the town deli. When you walked in the front door you were in the living room where my mom slept on a pull-out couch facing a dark wooden entertainment center that stretched to the ceiling. She decorated the walls with giant palm fronds that were prevalent in the 1970s, shaped like the spades and clubs in a deck of playing cards. To the right was the room I shared with my brother, who was a year and a half older than me. At night, I talked until my brother told me to shut up, or sang along with the radio the deli owner always played when he was cleaning up and closing for the night.

One morning, when my mother went to the neighbor's house next door to talk, my brother and I grabbed her basket of thread and, spool by spool, crisscrossed the entire living room, daring each other to find a way around the thread and to the front door. My brother and I jumped on tables and the back of the couch, wrapped thread around a macramé plant holder before whizzing to the other side of the room and connecting it to a doorknob. We called it Spiderweb City and were incredibly pleased with our work until Mom came home and yelled at us. She swung and hacked her way to the scissors she used to hack everything down; we were not allowed to go outside to play for a week. Pieces of navy blue thread floated from the dark wood of the entertainment center for weeks.

My grandma came over to get us ready for school in the morning when my mom had to go to work. In the winter, she turned on the oven and sat at the kitchen table smoking Carlton 120s, and read the paper while we brushed our teeth and fought over the bar of soap at the sink. When we were finished and came out to the kitchen, our clothes were already laid out for us, draped over the backs of two wooden chairs. My grandma opened the oven door and made us stand in front of it to get dressed. Sometimes she would turn on the radio and we would dance along to Van Halen (our choice) or the Four Tops (hers). When she walked us to school, she told us about what it was like when she was growing up in the city, how she used to jump from the roof of one building to another for fun, or fill bottle caps with wax and flick them with her fingers.

When my grandma told me about college, that when I got older I could go away to school and sleep there, I let go of her hand, stopped walking, and shouted, "I am *never* going to college! It sounds like *jail!*" I cried at the thought of leaving my mother. I protested many of the things she told me I could do when I grew up—I was absolutely not going to get married, and she was crazy if she thought I would ever have babies once I knew how they were made and where they came out of your body.

In school one day, someone outed me. As I stood in the cafeteria line clutching my green reduced lunch card, Thomas Scarfino poked the space between my shoulders and said, "Those are for poor people. You're poor!" He laughed and had his friends join him in taunting me, sing-songing, "Poooo-oor! Pooooo-oor! Danielle is poooo-oor!" until one of the monitors asked them to stop.

I knew that our milk at home came in a cardboard box instead of a plastic jug, and that the money in my mom's wallet was vivid like a coloring book instead of plain and green like you saw in the cash register in the deli, but I never knew we were poor.

I remember being happy. We had nothing you could measure in money, but we were happy with one another. Most children do not have stringent markers of time, but I know that my happiness ended, that my life with my family changed forever, the day my mom met the man who would become my stepfather.

They met in the city. One day we went school shopping at Macy's. He was buying sneakers, and my mother gave him her number though he hit on my aunt first. He took a bus to Greenwood Lake the following weekend and never left.

We suddenly had to move often. My mom would give him an envelope full of money to pay the rent, and he would drive to the city to buy drugs with it. We moved out of the apartment over the deli to a house near the lake. He was often gone at night, and home during the day. My mom had to walk to work, farther away now that we moved, because he had our car and usually left it without gas. When my mom worked at the restaurant at night he was supposed to watch us, but he took us with him to the city instead, over the Tappan Zee Bridge into the Bronx, where he was from. Sometimes we sat outside waiting for him in the car for a long time. I read Beverly Cleary books with a small plastic flashlight, or played cards with my brother until he came back. We kneeled on the ground where your feet were supposed to go, facing the trunk, our feet pushed under the front seats so that we had more room to play Matches, Slap Deck, or other games we made up. Big shadows crossed the window when people walked by; sometimes they looked in and saw two kids playing cards, looking back at them with scared eyes. My brother and I were tired at school now, since we stayed up late at night. We went to school with bruises, tender from where he grabbed our legs and arms to punish us when we ran inside the house, sore from when he punched us for asking if we were going to eat dinner that night. His eyes were always big, barely any white around the edges. His eyebrows were always raised, stretching to reach his hairline. We tried not to bother him, but we always got in his way no matter what we did, and it always made him mad.

They got married. They had children. He had a child from another relationship whom he thought he could do a better job of raising. His son, DeAndre, was seven when he came to stay with us, and he lived with us for four months before his father beat him for talking back to a teacher at school. When the ambulance came for DeAndre, the cops came, too, and told my mother that my stepfather had to stay 1,000 feet away from my brother and me when he got out of jail. My mother took us to my grandparent's house and moved to the Bronx with him. We did not see her again for years.

I don't know when my mom realized he was hitting us. Our bruises were visible, but we were active kids and denial is powerful. Surely we had become quiet, shut down from living in fear. Didn't she notice? My mom said she did not know that he would come into my room at night and stick his fingers inside of me, high on cocaine or crack or heroin, until I was sixteen, when I frightened my grandparents by trying to find ways to kill myself. One day they made me tell them why, and I did. My mom did nothing when she found out, even though my grandmother promised to cut his throat if he ever set foot in her house again, even though my mom was still married to him. The only thing I could do was to stop talking to my mother, so I did. I stopped trying to kill myself for a few years, and learned how to live in a world without her. No one understood why I lived with my grandparents, why I did not have a mom and a dad and a house like they did. I did not know how to tell them that living with a mom and a dad is not all it is cracked up to be. I held on to the shame of my messy upbringing for years.

In her book *Belonging: A Culture of Place*, hooks wrote, "Contemporary black folks who embrace victimhood as the defining ethos of their life surrender their agency." By the time I'd read that passage I had already found a way to save myself from the victimhood that threatened to swallow me whole on a daily basis, and her reinforcement kept it at bay.

When you grow up poor in an affluent town, anger becomes an easily accessible tool. Years of ridicule taught me to keep people at arm's length. I was mad, easily marked as such by my combat boots, black lipstick, partially shaved head, and limited tolerance for the people I sat in classrooms with day after day. Life with my grandparents was good, stable. I heard them worrying about whether or not they would ever be able to retire now that they were the legal guardians for my brother and me. We had food, beds, and safety for the first time in years, but I was angry with my mother for leaving, angry that I was stuck in a suburban town that would forever cast me as the villain just for having black skin and a keen mind, for being a young woman who stood up for her ideas and ideals. My way of dealing with not fitting in was to noticeably *not* fit in, to be sure the way I looked on the outside prevented anyone from even trying to get to know what I was like on the inside.

This sort of rebellion may be typical of some suburban kids. Talk to a teenager at the mall and you may get a similar story of angst and the deliberate personal expression of it. But it felt like the stakes were higher for me. I was not just a weird kid, but also a weird black kid, which threw off the assumptions people had about how I should act.

I read bell hooks's *Where We Stand: Class Matters* during the summer between my sophomore and junior year of college. She described her life in a way that made sense to me, and I related deeply to how she described coming to class consciousness through her working-class family. Since I refused to think of myself as a victim, I did not understand that I was, in fact, a victim of classist culture. It did not matter how I acted or what I did, since there were already cultural predictors in place affecting how people thought of poor, black women. If I failed in life, it would be expected, since I started with nothing. If I succeeded, I was the shining product of a brilliant meritocratic system, even though that system did very little to address my personal needs.

hooks made it possible for me to think of myself as more than poor, black, and female—and how these collective components create a different set of cultural expectations for me. Mrs. Dieder did not engage with me as an intellectual child because she did not expect me to be one, having learned how "those kinds of people" act and approaching her classroom with all of those prejudices firmly intact. When I read bell hooks, I started to think about my role in the world, and my life outside of my small town. I started to identify structural issues that contributed to the low expectations people had of me, our historically racist approach to public education and access to higher education that contributed to educational roadblocks even in the 1990s. She gave me permission to question our investment in a biased system, and simultaneously encouraged me to find the people who would bolster my interest in leveling the playing field, particularly now that I knew they were out there.

No one in my family identifies as a feminist even though they all seem to be committed to gender equality and civil rights. As a result, I discovered feminism by accident.

I always watched the news with my grandmother, a nightly lead-in to our mutual love of *Jeopardy!* and *Wheel of Fortune*. She sat on the multicolored striped couch puffing away at her Calrton 120s, and I parked myself on the floor to sew or crochet somewhere below the smoke line. Like a lot of families, we thought of the news as an active participatory event, and we looked forward to talking to the television and, subsequently, to each other. "Ugh, that Madonna," my grandmother would say when news of her current tour or latest media spectacle would flash across the screen. "Who needs her? She can't even sing." We commented on everything from war to fluctuating New York City crime statistics to the dynamic between anchors Sue Simmons and Chuck Scarborough (riveting). We talked about the world, and got worked up about marginalized groups being further marginalized.

My grandmother used the stories of the world to paint a picture of how she wanted my life to turn out, saying "Don't ever let someone tell you that you can't be president just because you're a woman" or "You have to stand up for yourself—did you see the way that man just interrupted and talked all over that lady? Never let someone disrespect you that way." "If you are out walking around by yourself at night, carry a knife—if someone messes with you, stab first, ask questions later. Nobody prosecutes these assholes that go around abusing women. Go to jail with a smile on your face."

Not all of her advice was fantastic. But it was important to my grandmother that I feel like I could move through the world with confidence, especially since she knew how much I was struggling in school. She never mentioned the word "feminism" in my presence, but she showed me in her own way the importance of personal and political conviction rooted in feminist ideals. It opened me up to finding out about feminism the way most of us did in the early 90s— through *Sassy* magazine.

I bought a subscription to *Sassy* with my babysitting money after I picked up a copy at the five-and-dime one day after school. Buried on the rack behind *Teen Beat* and *Seventeen*, *Sassy* promised to live up to my nonconforming aesthetic from cover to cover. They talked about the music I loved, and the clothes I wanted, and they talked about feminism. I went to the dictionary to look up what it meant, and immediately decided that *yes*, that is what I am. I am a feminist!

I came of age in the riot grrrl era, and it served me well. I try to explain how amazing it was to grow up in a decade where the word "feminism" was not a pejorative, where you regularly heard women discussing issues like abortion and safer sex in mainstream media outlets, where even schmaltzy teen shows like *Beverly Hills, 90210* tried to have a feminist edge from time to time. Through feminism I found a way to effect change in my own life. I found my political voice and started clubs in school. I took charge of my education by deciding to apply for college despite what my high school teachers thought of my prospects and, when I got accepted, moved to Boston to try my luck.

It wasn't what I expected. I could not see myself reflected in the classroom or culture; it was taken for granted that the canon did not include women of color, and that it was selfish to ask for inclusion. When the first year was over and summer rolled around, I dropped out and moved to California with $200 in my pocket.

Feminism helped me connect to the part of myself I'd been told was too much—too loud, too picky, too out of place. Now I had something to point to and say, Nope, you're wrong, and a lot of other women before me have felt the same way. In California, I was completely on my own, but I had never felt more confident.

After several years, a number of restarts of my life in various cities, I landed in Rhode Island and enrolled in an introduction to women's studies course. Three weeks later, I was reading bell hooks for a homework assignment.

The professor only assigned one essay from *Feminist Theory: From Margin to Center*, but I went to the library and checked out the entire book. I read it in one sitting. Then I went to the local bookstore and purchased it. I read it again, this time highlighting passages and folding down corners of the pages so frequently that the front cover always rests slightly open. Nothing had ever made as much sense to me. hooks's insistence that we need a feminist theory that speaks to everyone in order to effect revolutionary change was now the basis of my academic career. When hooks wrote about how systems of power affected the development of a culture rooted in gender equality, it was like she was handing the world a blueprint for ending sexism. And when hooks wrote, "I am suggesting that [black women] have a central role to play in the making of feminist theory and a contribution to offer that is unique and valuable," I felt all of the validation and hope the riot grrrl movement was never quite able to give me.

Even though I am no longer in school, I continually reference this text. There are more times when I feel out of place than there are that I feel included, and it's nice to be able to pick up a book, read a few paragraphs, and remind myself that the work I am committed to doing is necessary, that I can make a feminist space in places where one does not seem to have developed naturally. I think about bell hooks often, and reflect on how she has come to be iconic to me even though her work was absent from my life for more than half of it.

Instead of being ashamed of where I come from, instead of hiding my broken life in an attempt to fit in with what I thought an academic looked like, I've instead decided to use the pain, to become a person invested in helping others access their power through thought and action. With hooks, I learned how to trust my instincts, and that it is okay to question everything. I learned how to trust my struggle, that the chaos of my childhood still managed to produce an intelligent and stable person who has surrounded herself with love.

hooks is the person who revealed the secret of academia to me, which is that when you use your own language, when love and passion are part of your work, you are able to reach more people. And isn't that why we are in this business, to reach people? To be part of their process of growing and changing? Isn't that what we look for in every job, in every conversation?

In my life before I found bell hooks's work, I did not understand how to distance myself from the parts of my family that broke me. The messages I received were about the importance of family, not the way they can break you down or cause strife. Like hooks, I had grown up hearing that "Family is more important than friends," but I had no idea what to do with that since my family had failed me so completely. I had to go really far out to come back in. I had to learn how to use tools in a way that worked for me, and that it was okay to want to break down the system from within. I had to be confident and protective of what

I loved. Having discovered hooks late in my life, I was able to look at a sizeable portion of her career to see that she, too, has moved to a place of love. She writes about love and acceptance openly, even though some have criticized her for moving away from the dense academic notions that are the typical model for what a professor should be doing at this stage in her life. She is still bucking the system, favoring her whole life instead of one facet of it.

The Mrs. Dieders of the world are still telling black children that they are not worthwhile. Black girls and women are still looking for a schematic that could be helpful to them when they decide to break out of the restrictive societal roles we've created for women of color. I went to graduate school to be a teacher. Even though I'm not teaching as a career, I still teach. I'm in a position to encourage people to find their outlet and hold on to what they love most about themselves. I am often able to encourage people to go forward with love, but still fight like a motherfucker for everything they believe in. I encourage people in my life to find someone who is doing exactly what they want to do, and to see a path for themselves in their footsteps. I found that in bell hooks. Maybe someone will find it in me.

DANIELLE HENDERSON's work has been featured in various publications including *The Guardian*, *Vulture*, and *Cosmopolitan*. She created *Feminist Ryan Gosling* before leaving academia forever.

JUSTIN VIVIAN BOND

on

KAREN GRAHAM

Recently I had a birthday. I seem to have one every year. This year I decided to get myself something really nice. At first I couldn't decide what it should be, and then I realized what I wanted was to have my chart read by a woman I had been following on the internet for years. Twice a month she wrote new moon and full moon blogs, which I read religiously. At the end of every blog she wrote, "Why not treat yourself to a Jungian dream analysis?" I'd been in Jungian analysis for many years and this time I thought, "Perfect! What a special treat to have this woman, an expert in Jungian psychology, interpret my chart."

Jungian philosophy is one in which you are supposed to be put in contact with your subconscious mind. Some people might call it your unconscious mind. In my case that is more apt. I've been very tapped into my unconscious mind for quite some time now. So much so that often times I don't feel like I have to think at all.

The psychic told me that she saw a lot of "cat" energy around me, and she surmised that in a former life I might have been a guard at the temple of Dendur. I thought that sounded like something I might enjoy doing; in fact, even in this life I'd been raised in church. In any case, she said

I seemed like the kind of person who would protect cats. That much is certain. I do love cats, and I've always had cats around me. My cat Pearl and I have a very close relationship and, come to think of it, I do have a lot in common with cats. You know how common it is see a cat staring at a wall? I've heard people say so often, "I wonder what that cat is thinking about." Well I can tell you exactly what cats are thinking about. They are thinking about nothing. They are not thinking anything at all. And the reason I know that is because I do the same thing. I keep one entire wall of my bedroom completely blank so I can stare at it and not have to think about anything including what's on it. Sometimes I don't want to think, I just want to sit and look at a wall. It's the way I am. In a strange way it makes me feel pretty. Is that bizarre? I read somewhere that models practice a blank middle-distance stare. That in order to look truly at ease you have to clear your mind and see nothing so the viewer can project anything they want onto you.

Which reminds me of how I spent a lot of my time as a kid. I would look at fashion magazines. My absolutely favorite model was the one for Estée Lauder. She was blank and sphinx-like, only more modern because she was wearing *lots* of makeup. I decided that with enough makeup on you could convince anybody of anything. So I stared at her for hours on end and convinced myself that one day I would be seen as the person I knew myself to be—but until then I had to hide her in order to survive. All I had to do was to wait, and believe, and keep staring straight ahead at the future. *She*, the vision of blank perfection in the Estée Lauder ads, assured me I would become the person I am today.

In high school I tore every advertisement I could find with her image on it out of magazines. I tore them out of *Vogue*, *Harper's Bazaar*, and *Town & Country*. In the storage closet of the art classroom in my high school there were stacks and stacks of magazines. I went through every page of every one of them. I went to the local library and checked out magazines and ripped through them, trying to find this one particular model. By the time I graduated from high school I had a thick stack of Estée Lauder ads and mailers for Estée Lauder creams and scents from The Bon Ton, our local "high end" department store.

I had spent more time looking at her face than probably any face before or since. I drew her in pencil and pastel; I painted her in watercolor, acrylic, and oil. The first piece of art I ever had in a museum was a pastel drawing I did of the Estée Lauder model, which was included in a show of notable artworks from local high school students at The Washington County Museum of Fine Art in my hometown. The first painting I sold was a painting of her, a watercolor I sold to the local electric company, Potomac Edison. I won blue ribbons at the county fair—ribbons in both the youth and adult categories—for pictures I had done of her. I stared into her face and saw a gleaming smile with impenetrable, dead eyes. I've been trying to replicate that detached, dead-eyed smile for my entire life. Nothing is more appealing to me than a dead-eyed smile. It's all I've ever aspired to, a kind of dispassionate engagement, which is calculated, informed, and unperturbed. Her dead-eyed smile says, "I'm smiling at you because I'm cognizant that this is appropriate behavior even if I feel nothing. What I'm doing I'm choosing to do with intention."

My mother used to ask me all the time, "Why that woman?" "What is it about her?" "Why do you always have to look at that woman's face?" And all I could come up with was, "Because she looks SERENE!" That's all I wanted in my life, a little piece of mind, serenity, detachment—to escape into an image I could create of myself and for myself. I wanted to live in that state of grace.

Having grown up under the unflinching gaze of the gender police at home and in the streets, all I wanted was to escape—to be able to express myself as I was or as I wished to be. The Estée Lauder model was the quintessential aspirational white woman of elegance, pictured as she was in perfect eye makeup and perfect teeth, whether in a perfectly clinical setting, clean and unsoiled, or in an elegant home surrounded by Ming vases and Chippendale furnishings.

According to the Estée Lauder ads, this woman only read out of doors where she was pictured on the moors of Scotland holding a bouquet of heather in one hand and a book in the other, or when she stood starkly in a white dress against a privet, with a letter in her hand having carelessly dropped the envelope to the ground. What could that letter have said? Who could it have been from?

Maybe she never actually read at all; she wasn't actually looking at either the book or the letter. She was staring blankly off into the middle distance. Maybe she was struggling with some kind of moral dilemma as to whether or not to follow her heart or her commitments to home, family, and tradition. So much to think about . . . and yet it seemed the only place she could find the space and time to read or think was when she was out of doors, away from her pottery wheel where she was pictured confidently at work on a bust of one of her children, or next to her bathtub where she was only photographed in a robe, high heels, and stockings. She certainly wasn't allowed to let her mind wander when she was in the dermatologist's office prepping for the latest Estée Lauder skin treatment with hairdryer tubes swinging around behind her, adding an aura of the ultra-modern cleanliness and whiteness. No, it was only on a park bench in a plaid skirt with a nosegay in one hand and a book in the other that she could attain any measure of intellectual freedom, but still the camera of Victor Skrebneski, relentless in its drive for perfection, remained focused on her and she on it.

At the time, I wanted so badly to get the hell out of my parents' house and the stifling small-town mentality in which I was raised. I knew I could never be who I was meant to become there, that I would never be seen for whom I truly was until I was far, far away. So until I could make my move toward freedom I escaped into movies and magazines.

The astrologer reading my chart said, "Well, I guess I don't need to tell you but you've got a very difficult chart!"

I said, "Oh, of course!" as if I knew this. I didn't want her to think I had one of those unexamined lives, as if I didn't know anything about myself. I nodded my agreement in a sly, casually knowing way, "Oh yes, of course, very difficult."

She said, "You've got two grand crosses in your chart."

"Does that mean I was born double-crossed?"

"Basically."

I was born on a full moon with the sun in Taurus, the moon in Scorpio, and my rising sign in Cancer. I was also born with Mercury in retrograde. I've heard many people joke that between their period and PMS they only have about four good days a month. Well, I've only got about three good weeks every quarter because Mercury is only in retrograde three weeks out of every quarter of the year. That's my time. I can't help but think that while most people have all those other weeks to be happy and get themselves sorted out, I've got to get busy when Mercury is in retrograde, which makes my good days limited, but probably better than most.

So anyway, this psychic started telling me all these things about myself and I half-listened, focusing on how best to respond in order to get the most out of her, coaching myself with thoughts like, "Ask questions so you seem engaged . . . Try to be insightful about yourself . . . Quick, say something . . . Keep her talking . . ." I took a lot of notes and afterward I played the whole recording back. I was surprised by what I heard: She had asked me an awful lot of questions. Shouldn't she have been more declarative? I didn't need more questions. I wanted answers!

Once again I was left to my own devices. What else could I do? I boarded an airplane and began to stare off into the vast nothingness before me—but my joyous vacancy kept getting interrupted by the myriad questions the questionable psychic had peppered me with. I thought, "Oh Goddess! Here I go again, forced into bearing even more involuntary thoughts." *Sometimes I just don't want to think!* Finally I had to ignore the space in front of me and go inward. Terrifying!

On this particular day I was on a flight to California. I had already flipped through *Vogue* and *Harper's Bazaar*, reading a few articles on the stiflingly myopic lives of the rich and famous. After having compared myself favorably to their desperate foibles, I settled in for a bit of self-examination. One of the questions the psychic had asked me was, "What do you crave?" It took me a long time to come up with an answer to that one. After a couple of hours of thinking, meditating, and staring, the only two things I could come up with were oysters and beautiful surroundings. I've always enjoyed oysters because they seem glamorous and adult. When I was a child at Thanksgiving we had regular stuffing and stuffing with oysters in it. The oyster dressing was the dressing that the adults got to eat, so I couldn't wait until I was old enough for that one. And every now and then my mother would fry oysters to make sandwiches, which I didn't actually like, but which I did enjoy eating because they made me feel like a grown-up. It wasn't until I got older that I discovered that you could eat oysters raw. Although it was disgusting at first, at a certain point it made me feel like I was infusing my spirit with the waters of Oshun. Eventually my love of the oyster became elevated to the spiritual.

I read the book *Tipping the Velvet*, about a working-class lesbian who dressed as a man and came from a family of oyster people. So I guess eating oysters also makes me feel a bit like a cross-dressed lesbian, which is something everyone should experience for themselves if they can. I've dated many cross-dressed lesbians. I was even married to one, but I've never actually felt like one myself until I'd read *Tipping the Velvet* and went on an oyster rampage. From that day on, I resolved to eat more oysters, which seemed completely doable.

But as for the beautiful surroundings, I started to think that that might be problematic. At the time, I was living in a loft on Second Avenue above a very disreputable hole-in-the-wall bar called Mars Bar. They played loud music, all of it wonderful, old-school, downtown New York punk. The place stank to high heaven, like the ghost of dead junkies who were left to rot in their own piss. My bedroom was directly above the bathroom, which I am quite sure acted as a shooting gallery for the few junkies and speed freaks who were left in New York City. Some people might have thought they were a pestilence—the junkies and speed freaks—but to me they were all we had left. However, they did not contribute to an aura of sweetness, and ultimately I was forced to duct-tape all the cracks in my walls and floors, and stuff quilts in holes to keep the stench from coming into my shabby, chic boudoir. It was sort of like living in Green Acres, only instead of a farm outside it was a crack den. It was interesting, it was fun, but I wouldn't call it beautiful.

Sadly, my time in Crack Acres was coming to an end because the building was scheduled for demolition. All of its inhabitants as well as the cockroaches and cokeheads at Mars Bar were being forced to evacuate to make way for a new steel and glass condominium tower which was part of the Avalon development project going up between Second Avenue and Bowery. Avalon had already been responsible for the destruction of McGurk's Suicide Hall on Bowery, where in the 1890s Bowery prostitutes would go to commit suicide. It is a storied block. I had heard tales of murders in my own hallway too gruesome to go into here. The building had been homesteaded by Ellen Stewart and other members of the La Mama family in the late 1970s. Across the hall from me lived John Vaccaro, one of the founders of the Ridiculous Theatrical Company, who had worked with Charles Ludlam and Jackie Curtis and a bevy of downtown legends in 1960s. In an odd way, John reminded me of my Pappy in that he was nasty, rude, and mean, but he had so much fun being that way you couldn't help but get a kick out of him.

Fortunately, because I did get a kick out of him, he liked me and would come over and share stories about working with Jackie Curtis, who is a personal hero of mine, and show me pictures of my trancestors in their youthful glory, when their courage, outrageousness, and heavy drug usage paved the way for the life of relative acceptance that I am able to enjoy now.

The last party in my loft took place on gay pride weekend. The Monday afterward I put my things in storage and went on the road for six months. By the time I found myself on that airplane, post-psychic reading, the luxury of stability and beautiful surroundings was indeed something I craved.

Finally, in February of the following year, I moved into my current apartment on East Twelfth Street and began feathering my nest. What do you crave? Oysters and beautiful surroundings. After returning from California I ended the tour supporting my second record, *Silver Wells*, with a concert on Fire Island in the Cherry Grove Community Center. A gay couple I knew said, "You must come out to Sag Harbor sometime." I'd never been to Sag Harbor, but I knew it was an enclave (I just love the word "enclave." It makes me think of naked bohemians running around Laurel Canyon or tubercular artists living in Giverny; some sort of wild and privileged gated community where the rich and talented make all of their mistakes in private). I thought to myself, that sounds like beautiful surroundings so I said, yes I'd love to. I'd spent enough time around dirty queers; I'd spent enough time waking up in tents, surrounded by spilt lube bottles with amyl nitrate spills which had burned their way through tent floors, and seeped into the topsoil, leaving despoiled earth in its wake. I needed to up the ante and start hanging out with some nice-smelling bourgeois homosexuals. Don't get me wrong; I love the dirty queers; they're my people. But on occasion it's nice to wake up on a firm mattress surrounded by expensive knicky-knacks. It was time for me to engage with a different class of people, to broaden my horizons, and step into a land of high thread-counts and designer wallpaper.

On the appointed day, I got on the Jitney to Sag Harbor where my friends have a beautiful home on one of the main streets downtown. After putting down my suitcase they gave me a tour of their home and gave me my pick of any of the guest rooms. The top floor was the attic, which had a rustic charm and beautiful wooden eaves. I noticed that on the bed there was an Hermès blanket and I thought, "This is where I shall sleep tonight!" Even though it was ninety-six degrees and there was no air conditioning in that attic, I resolved that since this might be my one chance to sleep under a Hermès blanket by God I was going to sleep under it! So I turned on the charming vintage Westinghouse fan, which sat atop a beautiful antique marble table next to a sculpture of a laughing cupid, crawled under the Hermès blanket, and slept better than I can remember having ever slept in my adult life. What had I been thinking all those years curled up with goat boys in tents on beds of moss in the wilderlands of Canada, Tennessee, and Northern California? Clearly, a Hermès blanket under the eaves in Sag Harbor was where I was meant to be!

In the morning I awoke, showered, and skipped downstairs in my finest chinoiserie to a breakfast of lemon buttermilk pancakes, warm maple syrup, fresh coffee, and fruit compote. While I was enjoying my repast, my host said, "I don't know if you'd be interested, but I farm oysters. Would you like to harvest some of my oysters with me this afternoon?" I sat bolt upright, shocked. At first I thought I was in some sort of twisted game, some sort of high-class bourgeois version of *Punk'd*. Was he kidding me? But I realized, no, everybody around here is sincere. I collected myself, reigning in my caustic cynicism, "Why yes, yes I would, I would like to go and farm oysters with you today."

"Well, we can either go around noon or in the afternoon, say, around four. Which would you prefer?"

Now I don't go into the direct sunlight. I don't do it. I don't enjoy it. I have listened to Noël Coward's tunes, I know all about mad dogs and Englishmen, and even though I'm not a mad dog, nor am I English, I still refuse to go out in midday sun. So I said, "Let's go later in the day. I think the four o'clock time would be perfect. Meanwhile, I am going downtown to do a little shopping."

I set out in an all-cotton, breezy ensemble with a hat to keep the sun out of my eyes, feeling very white-woman-of-elegance and headed to downtown Sag Harbor. As I made my way around consignment and antique shops and stores with any and all kind of pickled and exotic canned goods, jams, sundries, I came across a stationery store. That's just what I need! I went in thinking, I have got to find the perfect stationery to let people know who I am and what I stand for as an aspirational white woman of elegance. This is ground zero, a place for me to begin defining myself and my new role in life. I spent hours in there. I thought, Should I get stationery that has a "V" on it? Or should I get stationery that has a "B" on it? I think it would be more traditional to have my last name; "B" for Bond. But then I thought, No, use "V" for Vivian, to celebrate the declaration of my new identity as a transperson, "V" as my pronoun of choice. But then I thought, Maybe that's too obvious, maybe I should have something more subtle, something more elegant or whimsical. It was so confusing.

I spent hours and hours until I finally settled on note cards with a ladybug and a leaf, since I'm a dendrophile, which is also the name of my first record. I left the store very proud of my new stationery. It wasn't until I got home that I realized what I was really declaring was that I was a sentimental thirteen-year-old girl! Fortunately, I know enough goofy people I could send those cards to that it doesn't really matter. I'm sure lots of people would be delighted to accept me as a sentimental thirteen-year-old girl. I'm lucky that way.

I made my way back to my friend's house because it was

getting to be time to harvest the oysters. I was trembling with excitement. We loaded up the station wagon and made our way down to the harbor where my friend kept a charming little red motorboat. As we were unloading the station wagon I noticed a pair of waders. I said, "Are we going to be wearing those?" He said, "It's not necessary because in August the water is not that cold but if you would like to wear waders you certainly can."

I said, "Yes I would like to wear waders. That sounds fantastic." So we put the waders in the boat and made our way through the harbor past the yachts and all of the expensive people, places, and things. He took me to a place where there were rows of rope coming out from the shore, which were, as it turned out, his oyster beds. I excitedly slipped into the waders and put on my round l.a. Eyeworks sunglasses, the ones that make me feel like Joan Didion in the photo on the back cover of *Slouching Towards Bethlehem*, and stood there in the water going blank. I was frozen like a statue.

"Would you like to help?" he said.

Now ordinarily I'm not a helpful person. I don't like being helpful. It's a terrible thing to have to admit, but it's true. I've heard many people at a dinner party or at a luncheon say, "Is there anything I can do to help?" So I say it, too, but I always silently pray they will say, "No thanks. Just sit and enjoy your cocktail."

When I was in college I was hired by the costume department to do my work-study hours there, in spite of the fact that I did not know how to sew and that I knew nothing about costume construction. I didn't even know how to do a load of wash. But what I did know was how to gossip. So they would give me some fake cherries, a hat, a needle and thread, whatever, and I would sit for hours and gossip while I made gestures toward the hat as if I was going to sew those cherries on it so that someone would end up with a fantastic period hat to wear in a production. I never did get the cherries attached, but I certainly made the time go by for the others.

But when my friend asked if I wanted to help harvest the oysters, I had a feeling of genuine enthusiasm such as I had never experienced before. "Yes! I would like to help!" I wanted to help very much, indeed. I wanted to learn how to harvest oysters because oysters were one of the two things I craved in this life. Yes please, let me help!

So I grabbed a pair of blue Playtex Living gloves and a great big brush and I sloshed my way over to where the beds of oysters were waiting to be harvested. The oysters were in these big, plastic containers attached to ropes on a pulley system and they were covered with algae and scum. It was my job to take the brush and scrape off the algae from the plastic containers that had holes in them so that the water could flow in and out, and the oysters would be in fresh water at all times as they grew and multiplied. I scraped the algae off with the fervor of a newly minted fishwife.

Before I knew it I was standing there in the water with my Didionesque sunglasses on, the Playtex Living gloves overflowing with oysters in their shells, in waders, with the sun behind me shining down on beautiful clapboard houses of Sag Harbor—and for the first time I felt like I was where I truly belonged.

All of the sudden I had a flash! I flashed to an image of myself staring at a particular photograph of the Estée Lauder model. It was an image from a magazine ad campaign in 2000, when this model came out of retirement to promote a moisturizer for middle-aged women. In the photo she was standing in water, in waders wearing a plaid shirt with a hat on and holding a fly-fishing rod. All of the sudden, it was as if she and I were one and the same person. She had been someone I had aspired to be, someone I had admired and dreamed about, and fantasized and projected all my hopes and dreams onto, and all of a sudden, in middle-age I was in the same position as she was, with the same posture wearing the same outfit.

I said to my friend frantically, "take a picture, take a picture, take a picture!" I threw him my phone and he took a picture, and it was as if, for the first time in my life, everything was as it should be. It was as if I had been reborn into the image of myself I had always secretly carried within my imagination, but had never quite been able to achieve.

You see, I didn't know much about this Estée Lauder model, but I knew that she had been replaced in 1985 and I never saw an Estée Lauder ad I cared about again until 2000 when one day I was flipping through a magazine and there she was again—my model in a fly-fishing outfit. That was the last image I had seen of her. And here I was in almost the exact same outfit in Sag Harbor. For a moment, I wasn't sure who I was. Was I my model? Or was I myself?

When I got back to the house in Sag Harbor, and after consuming twice my weight in oysters, I settled in under the eaves, beneath the Hermès blanket. Suddenly it occurred to me that it was no longer 1985 or 2000; we are living in the age of the Internet. I grabbed my iPad and google-imaged the model whose name I had discovered years ago in a book of photographs by Skrebneski, a name that was profound in its unbridled WASPiness: Karen Graham. It was as if I had found a treasure trove filled with gold coins at the bottom of the ocean. Image after image of Karen Graham appeared before me, including the picture that had appeared seemingly out of the blue in 2000 when she was dressed as I had been dressed earlier that day. It was as if I were being reunited with a long-lost lover!

After exhausting myself looking at her still images, another miracle happened. I found a video! I'd never seen her in motion before, and the idea of seeing her in a video was almost too much for me to bear. And yet there she was in a video made by the English fashion photographer, Nick Knight. Evidently Knight had shot a video series called More Beautiful Women as an homage to Andy Warhol on the occasion of the millennial celebration of *British Vogue* and one of the models he videotaped was Karen Graham.

He asked each of the models to pose against a white

backdrop for two minutes without telling them what it was for or giving them any instructions on what to do. Every model revealed herself in one way or another. Alek Wek, the Sudanese-born British model, stood perfectly still for two solid minutes. Carmen Dell'Orefice, the septuagenarian goddess, took that opportunity to make a PSA about breast cancer awareness and gave herself a breast examination. But Karen Graham simply stared and occasionally smiled or moved her head ever so slightly all the while looking very uncomfortable as if she were waiting for some instruction from the photographer or a reason to be there until one minute and eight seconds into it, when she utters rather vaguely, in a clear, feminine voice with a lilting southern drawl, "Two minutes is a long time . . ." Two minutes is a long time! At the end of the two minutes she said thank you, walked away, and has never modeled or been heard from again.

I needed to know more. I began researching Karen Graham and discovered some basic facts from *Wikipedia*. She was born in Gulfport, Mississippi in 1945. She studied French at Ole Miss, the bastion of education for the old-school southern gentility, and later attended the Sorbonne in Paris. After graduating, she moved to New York, where she hoped to become a French high school teacher. While looking for a position, she went shopping at Bonwit Teller, and on her way down the stairs bumped into Eileen Ford, who gave her a modeling contract. She went on to appear on the cover of *Vogue* over twenty times, putting her in second place for most *Vogue* covers of all time. By 1973, she signed to become Estée Lauder's exclusive spokesmodel. She retired in 1985 at the age of forty while she was still on top. From then on she stayed out of public eye until making her one final brief appearance in 2000, when she appeared in Estée Lauder's Resilience Lift face cream in an ad campaign aimed at "mature" women.

Her personal life remains very private except for a few details, which appeared as headlines. In 1974, she was engaged to be married to the British TV personality David Frost. But she left him at the altar when, according to Lee Israel in *Estée Lauder: Beyond the Magic*, Delbert Coleman, the owner of the Stardust Hotel in Las Vegas, flew to London with a great big diamond and persuaded her to marry him. Coleman was allegedly involved in many shady real estate deals on the Nevada strip. According to *Beyond the Magic*, by 1980 Karen Graham was paid half a million dollars a year for thirty-five days of work. These biographical facts make me think Karen Graham could have been the heroine of a Sidney Sheldon or Harold Robbins novel, with such titles as *The Other Side of Midnight*, *A Stranger in the Mirror*, *Rage of Angels*, *The Naked Face*, or *Nothing Lasts Forever*. But it wasn't until after her retirement that I discovered that Karen Graham's story took on a more interesting dimension. What did she do with her time?

She left the city and moved upstate to Rosendale, New York, where she opened a fly-fishing school—"Fly-fishing with Bert and Karen"—with a fisherman named Bert

Darrow. She has been there since except for her brief return to modeling in 2000. It was at that time she gave her only in-depth interview to Dan Fallon of *The Flyfishing Connection* entitled "The Butterfly and the Trout."

It was in this interview that Karen Graham finally began to reveal herself to me. I was floored. Karen Graham seemed to be describing my own childhood when she said, "I would spend almost every afternoon out in the woods near my house observing nature. I would build little homes for me out of moss, ferns, or straw. Many afternoons after school I would spend hours crouched on that old log peering into the green lagoon beneath me. I was fascinated with the tadpoles and slithering creatures. I was in trouble when I found out my uptown boyfriends' idea of an outdoor adventure was sitting around a swimming pool balancing a silver reflector to speed up his tan."

Uncanny! For all those years I'd been wondering, What is it about this woman? It was as if she were speaking for me. There was more to her than just the dead eyes and the smile.

In hindsight, it was as if she had been telegraphing to me that my dreams had value. Who I wanted to be and what I wanted to do with my life were possible, in spite of what anyone around me might say. And even today, as I continue to struggle with the conflicts inherent in being a social butterfly and performer versus my inner craving for rural solitude, I still feel compelled to express my gratitude by making myself available to the many strangers and friends who come to see me perform, that the "tadpoles and slithering creatures" who exist behind the facade remain and are of equal, if not greater, value to what their inspiration allows me to present. As Karen Graham once said, "I suppose one can't help becoming rather addicted to the finer things in life. It didn't take long after my first real modeling success in New York for me to understand the difference between hotdogs and caviar!"

Interestingly, Karen Graham became a supermodel at a time when a model's name did not appear on the ad with her. For fifteen years she was the face of Estée Lauder. Estée Lauder herself was quite pleased for people to think that Karen Graham and she were one and same person. But Estée Lauder's story was something else entirely. She was born Josephine Esther Mentzer in 1908 in Corona, Queens. Karen Graham was born thirty-eight years later in Gulfport, Mississippi. By the time Karen Graham modeled for her exclusively, Estée Lauder was in her mid-60s. Estée Lauder's legendary ambition and hard work had placed her at the pinnacle of the cosmetics business. Her ceaseless drive had taken her into a circle of friends that included such luminaries as the Duchess of Windsor and Princess Grace, along with socialites on the international party circuit. Estée was saying to women all over the world, This could be you, too.

As a small-town transperson, I was sure that what I wanted was to escape into a world of glamour and elegance, taste and refinement. I scoured books by famed interior designer Billy Baldwin, who, I found out later, was a gay man from Baltimore, Maryland, not far from where I grew up. Amazing to think of me as a child gazing into these books filled with environments designed by a queen from Baltimore and advertisements for beauty creams created by a Jewish lady from Queens, planning my dream house, my dream career, and my dream life. I went for it with the mantra, "Keep it pretty, keep it shallow, keep it moving." But as I grew older and my critical mind began to assess what really mattered, I found that my childhood dreams remained as shadows, which hover over me—part of my unconscious mind. I had seemingly moved on to a more worthwhile and enlightened existence yet all I really craved were oysters and beautiful surroundings.

Rediscovering Karen Graham took me back to a formative moment and gave me permission to put on my waders and step into a new dream: to redefine and rediscover my own path again.

Mx JUSTIN VIVIAN BOND is a multi-hyphenate artist and the author of *Tango: My Childhood, Backwards and in High Heels.*

ZOE PILGER

on

MARY GAITSKILL

S he was meeting a man she had recently and abruptly fallen in love with." So begins Mary Gaitskill's short story "A Romantic Weekend," published in the 1988 collection *Bad Behavior*. Beth is waiting on the street in a state of "ghastly anxiety" for a man who has promised to take her away for the weekend. But it seems he's stood her up.

In fact, he is watching her from across the street, eating a slice of greasy pizza. He is purposefully late. Her anxiety is "weirdly pleasing" to him. "He should probably just stay in the pizza place and watch her until she went away. It might be entertaining to see how long she waited. He felt a certain pity for her. He also felt, from his glassed-in vantage point, as though he were torturing an insect."

In her panic, Beth enters a flower shop. She wants to buy him flowers. "She had a paroxysm of fantasy. He held her, helpless and swooning, in his arms. They were surrounded by a soft ball of puffy blue stuff." The "puffy blue stuff" is an abstract vision of safety, a cocoon in which she and her lover can be protected from the world. But she has agreed to go away for the weekend on the mutual understanding that she is a masochist and he is a sadist. What lies ahead is sexual violence.

I first came across *Bad Behavior* when I was browsing in

Foyles bookshop on the Charing Cross Road in London. It was the end of 2007 and I was twenty-three, just graduated from university. I was looking for books by female authors that offered me something other than the chic-lit narrative of redemption through romantic love.

The front cover of the Vintage edition caught my attention: it shows a sepia photograph of a young woman wearing tight white trousers and a tight white T-shirt, lying on the floor face down. Her knees are slightly raised. She appears to be supplicating somebody or something. She is vital but she is begging. There is darkness above her.

I bought the book but I didn't read it for another three years; I have since read it many times. The subtlety and skill with which Gaitskill reveals the horror of contemporary dating mores influenced me greatly. Along with several other books—*The Second Sex* (1949) by Simone de Beauvoir, *The Ravishing of Lol Stein* (1966) by Marguerite Duras, *Blood and Guts in High School* (1978) by Kathy Acker, *The Driver's Seat* (1970) by Muriel Spark—*Bad Behavior*, and particularly "A Romantic Weekend," helped me to formulate the ideas that would become my first novel, *Eat My Heart Out*, published by Serpent's Tail in the UK (2014) and the Feminist Press in the US (2015).

Gaitskill's opening scene is a dramatization of power and powerlessness. "To make someone wait—the constant prerogative of all power," Roland Barthes writes in *A Lover's Discourse: Fragments* (1977). Beth's lover's feeling of "torturing an insect" recalls Erich Fromm's description of sadism in

The Art of Loving (1956): "The child takes something apart, breaks it up in order to know it; or it takes an animal apart; cruelly tears off the wings of a butterfly in order to know it, to force its secret."

Like Beth's lover, Fromm's sadistic child is compelled by a need to know "the secret" of the insect. As a mysterious being with seemingly magical, autonomous inner workings, it must be dissected in order to be understood. Sadism does not merely suggest the pleasure derived from inflicting pain on others, but the desire for "complete mastery over another person, to make of him a hapless object of our will . . . to become his God." As a Jewish émigré from Nazism, Fromm's ideas of sadomasochism were informed by his experience of the submission of the German people to Hitler. As an exile in the United States, he was likewise influenced by the submission of the American people to light entertainment.

Nor is masochism a simple complex. It suggests the pleasure derived from pain inflicted on the self, but also radical doubt: "The masochistic person, whether his master is an authority outside of himself or whether he has internalized the master as conscience or a psychic compulsion, is saved from making decisions, saved from the final responsibility for the fate of his self." Fromm points out that many of our conventional ideas of love are in fact masochistic: "It seems that there is no better proof for 'love' than sacrifice."

The art of sacrifice is historically feminine. The idea that women enjoy being hurt has often been used by men to justify hurting them. In her article, "The Bonds of Love:

Rational Violence and Erotic Domination" (1980), Jessica Benjamin argues that the normative masculine posture in Western capitalist democracies is sadistic, while the feminine posture is masochistic. These roles are culturally constructed rather than natural, but nonetheless powerful. In this light, "A Romantic Weekend" appears to be an allegory of the violence of gender itself.

Beth's lover is a subtle kind of sadist. He understands that cruelty is psychological as well as physical. He objectifies and therefore dehumanizes Beth not simply by beating her, but by negating her sense of self. At the beginning of the story, it appears that she wills such self-abasement. She feels "like an object unravelling in all directions."

He forces her into a state of neurotic passivity by doing nothing at all. The act of making her wait is banal yet authoritarian; she responds with increased romantic fervor. Her fantasy of "swooning in his arms" implies a loss of self. She is intoxicated by his absence, by the possibility that he won't appear. In her imagination, she transforms him into a god. She pictures herself not as a victim, bound and gagged, but as the heroine of a mass-produced romance novel, surrendering to the overwhelmingly strong embrace of man who is capable of controlling her.

What makes "A Romantic Weekend" so unsettling is the fact that Beth is ostensibly a free woman. Like the TV show *Sex and The City*, which came a decade later in the 90s, *Bad Behavior* documents the romantic and professional travails of women as they try to find their way in New York.

Many have artistic aspirations. They exist in the aftermath of the second wave women's movement of the 60s and 70s, caught, as Elizabeth Young suggests in *Shopping in Space: Essays on America's Blank Generation Fiction* (1994), between contradictory imperatives.

On the one hand, it seems they must be pleasing and passive in order to catch and tame a man. On the other, they must assert themselves in order to compete in the neoliberal meritocracy; indeed, in order to survive in the city at all. To borrow a phrase from the journalist Martha Gellhorn, they are "free like nothing quite bearable."

While the second wave women's movement enabled unprecedented access to employment and education, it seems that cultural attitudes are much slower to change. Beth is adrift in a decade marked by a backlash against feminism. As Young seems to suggest, Gaitskill's heroines show "the impossibility of internalizing such seismic social change within a short period." They embody "cruel cultural dilemmas." The demand to be passive in private life and active in public life causes a kind of "feminine" schizophrenia.

Another great dramatization of the act of waiting is Dorothy Parker's 1928 short story, "A Telephone Call," which consists of a woman's monologue as she waits by the phone for her lover to call her. "PLEASE, God, let him telephone me now," she laments. Soon her delirium rises: "If I didn't think about it, maybe the telephone would ring. Sometimes it does that. If I could think of something else. If I could think of something else." She resorts to superstitions, counting meaninglessly to a hundred, sending herself mad.

Due to the dating mores of the time that Parker was writing, a woman could not merely pick up the phone and call a man herself. To do so would be a predatory act, as April Middeljans explains: "The command to wait may also be reinforced by the social expectation that women desire to be desired, to be the object of a subject's love." The pressure to be passive prey forces the female narrator into a masochistic relinquishment of the self. "The real pride," says the narrator. "The big pride, is in having no pride."

Benjamin argues that while the feminine posture tends to dissolve all boundaries of the self, the masculine posture asserts too rigid boundaries. This is evident in *Fifty Shades of Grey* (2012). Anastasia Steele is part Harlequin heroine, breathless and compliant, and part chick-lit heroine, educated and enfranchised. Christian Grey is aloof and commanding. Her accomplishments don't get in the way of her willingness to become his sexual slave, however. "I need to know your limits, and you need to know mine," Christian tells her. "This is consensual, Anastasia."

The issue of consent is what underpins "A Romantic Weekend." Beth is seeking her own pain, emotional and sexual. She tells her lover: "I hope you are a savage." Her bedroom wall is adorned with "a pasted-up cartoon of a pink-haired girl cringing open-mouthed before a spire-haired boy-villain in shorts and glasses. Her short skirt was blown up by the force of his threatening expression, and her panties showed." The image is both childish and pornographic.

However, Beth cannot conceal her own complexity: "She was delicately morbid in all her gestures, sensitive, arrogant, vulnerable to flattery. She veered between extravagant outbursts of opinion and sudden, uncertain halts, during which she seemed to look to him for approval." From his position in the pizzeria across the street, her lover muses: "She had said that she wanted to be hurt, but he suspected that she didn't understand what that meant."

Barthes describes the act of waiting as historically feminine. While men went out into the world, women were confined to the domestic sphere. "It is Woman who gives shape to absence, elaborates its fiction," he writes. "For she has time to do so; she weaves and she sings." The classic model is Penelope, who wove a funeral shroud every day that she waited for Odysseus, and unraveled it every night. The pressure for women to be passive persists.

In *Eat My Heart Out*, I also wanted to explore the idea of waiting. I wrote the first draft very fast—in three months, at night. It only occurred to me later that I had written a reversal of the power dynamic that Gaitskill describes. Unlike Beth, my twenty-three-year-old protagonist Ann-Marie makes her lover wait for her.

The novel begins with Ann-Marie hanging around outside Smithfield meat market at five in the morning. She has been to a party nearby. She picks up a man called Vic, who is "freakishly tall." They arrange to meet the next night at eight outside Chalk Farm tube station.

Instead of waiting for Vic at the station, however, Ann-Marie positions herself at the first floor window of the waxing salon across the road: "The manager had told me that they were nearly closing," she narrates. "But I'd made my eyes look beseeching like a spaniel and the drowned aesthetic must have helped because she let me in."

Outside, "the rain was torrential; it obscured the stars." Ann-Marie watches the station entrance. When Vic turns up, she observes his discomfort. "Ten minutes had passed. Soon he would go. Would he go? I watched him reach upward to the void of sky; he seemed to plead with it. And then he was going . . ." At this moment, Ann-Marie runs down the stairs and exits the waxing salon: "I had lost sight of him; *Him*. I wanted Him more now, much more, since He was already leaving me."

Like Beth, Ann-Marie has invested Vic with the power of a god. But instead of deferring to his divine presence, she follows him over the bridge to Primrose Hill and jumps on his back—"He grunted, a stuck pig." They fall together onto the pavement. Ann-Marie whispers into his ear: "Sorry I'm late . . . This seems like a good moment to lay my cards on the table. You're my first date since I got out of a really long-term relationship."

By making Vic wait, Ann-Marie assumes the mascu-line sadistic posture. But at the moment that he leaves, she switches to the feminine masochistic posture. She feels overwhelmed by love at the prospect of his abandonment.

This resonates with Barthes's theory of love: "Amorous absence functions in a single direction, expressed by the one who stays, never by the one who leaves . . ." He goes on, "the other is in a condition of perpetual departure . . . by vocation, migrant, fugitive." The fact of being left by her lover forces her into a position of solitude, which enables the space of imagination to open up. Ann-Marie can only imagine that she is in love with Vic; it is only the idea of him that obsesses her.

Following a disastrous night of failed sex, this becomes clear. Ann-Marie immediately bombards Vic with emails and texts. She watches Beyoncé videos on a loop on YouTube, projecting her own love for Vic into the lyrics; she desperately hopes that cosmic signs offered to her by the universe promise that Vic will definitely call her. But his face fails to appear in the clouds above Clapham Common; the two white swans that she sees swimming in the pond, perfectly in love and symmetrical, turn out to be two filthy old plastic bags. In the words of Barthes, Ann-Marie becomes "an unglued image."

It is in the realm of images that the struggle for power between Beth and her lover takes place. When he tells her on the plane to Washington that she is not a sexual person, too cerebral, she calls to her mind an image of him "holding her and gazing into her eyes with bone-dislodging intent, thinly veiling the many shattering events that she anticipated between them."

Love emerges in Beth's imagination as that which is capable of—pleasurably—killing her. She wants to be shattered; it seems that she has absorbed the many violent metaphors for love: to be hit by a lightning bolt; to be lovesick, then heartbroken. The death drive, Thanatos, is bound up with Eros, the life drive, in many of our commonplace ideas of what romance should be. And it is to that idea that Beth relentlessly turns.

Beth's mental image of her lover "made her disoriented with pleasure. The only problem was, this image seemed to have no connection with what was happening now. She tried to think back to the time they had spent in her apartment, when he had held her and said, 'You're cute.'" The more that he insults and ridicules her, the more she clings to this myth of original oneness. He too is besieged by images. He imagines his Korean wife at home with her "pretty, birdlike finger gestures . . . [then] He thought of Beth, naked and bound, blindfolded and spread-eagled on the floor of her cluttered apartment. Her cartoon characters grinned as he beat her with a whip."

Beth's lover splits his fantasy life between two age-old female archetypes: the obedient wife and the lascivious whore. One serves him in the domestic sphere; the other in the sexual sphere. Both are instrumentalized; they have a function, a purpose, only in relation to his needs. "He managed to separate the picture of his wife and the original picture of blindfolded Beth and hold them apart. He imagined himself travelling happily between the two. Perhaps, as time went on, he could bring Beth home and have his wife beat her too. She would do the dishes and serve them dinner."

The ease with which Beth's lover compartmentalizes the two women also recalls Benjamin's argument that "the male posture of emphatic differences" is contrasted to the female posture of "merging at the expense of individuality." If her lover instrumentalizes her, she instrumentalizes herself. She becomes an object in her own mind for him, while losing herself. This sense of losing, of falling, is part of normative femininity. The culture encourages, if not demands it.

In "A Romantic Weekend," Beth is constantly attempting a symbolic kind of suicide. All of her gestures of love can be interpreted as gestures of self-annihilation, manifested in the smallest acts. Erasure of her self is what both she and he seek; it is the one thing on which they seem to agree. However, they both fail.

Here lies the brilliance of Gaitskill's story. "He thought: there is something wrong. Her passivity was pleasing, as was her silence and her willingness to place herself in his hands. But he sensed another element present in her that he could not define and did not like." This other element in Beth is her intelligence.

When they arrive in Washington and drive to his grandmother's ugly apartment, where they are due to spend the weekend, "He realized what had been disturbing him about her. With other women whom he had been with in similar situations, he had experienced a relaxing sense of emptiness within them that had made it easy for him to get inside them and, once there, smear himself all over their innermost territory until it was no longer theirs but his."

In Beth, however, he discovers, a "tangible somethingness." Her body is "hatefully self-possessed." He cannot mark her as his territory; when he bites her, she doesn't like it. She does not experience a masochist's thrill of exquisite pain, however; she experiences almost nothing at all. His effect on her is minimal. In this way, he is undone. "He didn't mind the somethingness; he rather liked it, in fact, and had looked forward to seeing it demolished. But she refused to let him do it. Why had she told him she was a masochist?"

Benjamin's analysis of the 1954 novel *Story of O* by Pauline Reage here seems relevant. O is a successful fashion photographer; she agrees to submit to ritualized sexual slavery at a chateau in Roissy on the request of her lover, René. Rather than desiring a fully submissive woman, René's pleasure depends on O's enfranchisement. It is her choice to submit; she submits because she loves him. She is a slave to love.

The masters at Roissy derive their sadistic pleasure from the marks they make on O, both physical and emotional. It is her sense of self, her somethingness to be destroyed, which compels them. Her bruised and beaten body registers their presence in the world. Their sense of presence, of themselves, is evidently precarious. They cannot believe in their own existence without the visible marks of violence that they leave on a woman's body.

"The effect we have on something or someone is a way of confirming our reality," Benjamin writes. "If our acts have no effect on the other, or if the other refuses to recognize our acts, we feel ourselves to be powerless. But if we act in such a way so that the other person is completely negated, there is no one there to recognize us." O's masters will harm her but not kill her; if she were dead, there would be no one there to recognize them.

Mutual recognition would point to a reciprocal relation based on equality. However, the masculine and feminine postures are, by definition, not equal. "The relationship contains an actor and an acted upon, a negator and a recognizer," Benjamin writes. "Like the couple in the cuckoo clock, one must always be out when the other is in; they never meet."

Here lies the tragedy. If men and women are to assume the postures demanded of them by culture at large, then equality is not possible. Only an asymmetrical relation, based on domination and submission, is possible. Benjamin argues that the fantasy of erotic domination and rational violence "surfaces as a vital theme of the contemporary pornographic imagination where women are regularly depicted in the bonds of love."

The sadistic imagery of contemporary pornography, whereby the woman is violated in order for the man to achieve pleasure, exists on a continuum with the conventions of Mills & Boon romance novels. Pornography is typically aimed at male pleasure; romance novels at female pleasure. They are flipsides of the same asymmetrical fantasy: of power, on the one hand, and powerlessness, on the other. Beth and her lover are embodiments of this polarization; he craves violent sex, she craves saccharine romance.

Both are trying to force the other into a pre-scripted, mass-produced fantasy. Benjamin writes: "This fantasy, which mingles love, control, and submission, also flows beneath the surface of 'normal love' between adults."

I first read Benjamin's article around the same time that I read "A Romantic Weekend"; both influenced the development of my thought on the link between romantic love and sadomasochism. It is important to distinguish between cultural representations of romantic love, which are entwined with traditional ideas of femininity, and true love. To argue that romantic love is culturally constructed does not suggest that true love can't exist. In fact, it is true love that is contaminated by such asymmetrical power relations.

As Fromm argues, "love is based on equality and freedom." And: "love is an action, the practice of a human power, which can be practiced only in freedom and never as the result of a compulsion." However, capitalism has subsumed love, "its place is taken by a number of forms of pseudo-love which are in reality so many forms of the disintegration of love."

It is with the hologram of pseudo-love that my protagonist Ann-Marie is fighting. At once subject to it and resisting it, at once willing to give up all her power to a man, and defending what little power she has at all costs. She sighs to Vic on their first date: "Real men are hard to find." But the root of Ann-Marie's desire for romantic submission is existential. She is seeking refuge from her own freedom; in Fromm's words, she is suffering from "a fear of freedom."

While there are countless novels by male authors with male protagonists whose neuroses are considered an exploration of the complexity of the human condition, more often the troubles of female protagonists by female authors are relegated to the sphere of the "merely" personal. The latter is not considered a philosophical category of experience, but the stuff of thinly veiled memoir, confessionalism, narcissism. It is not invested with the grandeur of a crisis of faith, provoked by a dissolution of moral certainty. Rather, it is perceived as angst.

The fact that Ann-Marie has broken up with her long-term boyfriend is not the principal cause of her spiral into insanity. Sebastian, like Vic, is a cipher, a tabula rasa onto which she can project her own romantic fantasies. She is in love with the memory of Sebastian, but in reality she finds him absurd. The void which she experiences is historically specific: Ann-Marie has benefitted from all the gains of generations of feminists before her. She is educated and alone; she can do anything she wants. And so she goes crazy.

Repeatedly, she says that her freedom is a burden. She tells her date Dave toward the end of the novel, "I don't want to feel free . . . I want to feel constrained by something that's not evil, something that I can trust." Ann-Marie distrusts the permissiveness that surrounds her; she is in search of boundaries. At the same time, she abhors all boundaries. She is a contradiction. The dark humor of the novel is largely reliant on Ann-Marie's paradoxical thinking. She says: "I only ever want what I hate." The attraction/repulsion that she feels for men is expressed as violence.

While Beth endures physical harm without retaliating, Ann-Marie is pure aggression: she grinds her cigarette out on Vic's naked chest, and gives him a concussion. When he fails to reply to any of her emails, she turns up at his house at five in the morning and forces herself on him, persuading him not to use contraception. She gives him what she thinks he wants in the most violent manner possible: "I made my mouth into a black hole of suction." It was my intention to reverse the traditional power dynamic of female submissive/male dominant, and instead cast Ann-Marie as a pursuer.

Her behavior is the opposite of that which is advised by *The Rules*, updated by Ellen Fein and Sherrie Schneider in 2013 for "the digital generation." *The Rules* preaches extreme feminine passivity as a way to catch and keep a man: "the natural order of dating: the guy pursuing the girl." As a female pursuer, Ann-Marie is an aberration, akin to Glenn Close's character Alex Forrest in the 1987 film *Fatal Attraction*.

Indeed, Vic tells Ann-Marie that she is a "bunny-boiler," a term which entered common parlance after Forrest famously boiled a pet bunny in the film. Despite her confusion, Ann-Marie is keenly attuned to the fact that the personal is political, that even the smallest acts of love and sex express broader power structures. She says: "Someone's got to get fucked, and I'm pretty sick to death of it being me."

Beth seems to be searching for an authority to which she can submit in lieu of any certain position in society. Her desire to be tied up and beaten by a man points to a need for both physical restraint and punishment. It is as though the ritualized violence of sadomasochistic sex offers an antidote to her freedom. The punishment she asks for seems to be administered by the culture itself, reprimanding its female subjects for stepping out of line and demanding so much freedom. It is a plea for punishment for being free.

This is only tacitly expressed, and fails in its execution. Following their botched attempts at sadomasochistic sex, Beth contemplates her lover: "In the ensuing silence it occurred to her that she was angry, and had been for some time."

The conversion of passivity into rage is what distinguishes Beth's submissiveness from that of Anastasia in *Fifty Shades*. It was rage that I intended to impart to Ann-Marie too, albeit lacking a fixed target. Ann-Marie's explosive anger is a consequence of a general injustice that she feels all around her.

When I first began writing fiction, before I had conceived of the character of Ann-Marie, two lines from John Berryman's *The Dream Songs* (1969) recurred in my imagination. Somehow, they formed the abstract basis of the kind of young woman I wanted to create.

The first line was: "We're in business . . . Why / what business may be clear. / A cornering." The notion of a cornering by an agency that seems diffuse yet total is what I imagined Ann-Marie responding to. Her anger is a result of her feeling that she has been cornered. She doesn't know what has cornered her, or even how, but she can feel it, and she's lashing out. She's fighting with the power available to her, what Pierre Bourdieu calls "the weapons of the weak." She seduces men and dominates them; she is seduced and dominated. Never is she an equal.

The second line is the epigraph of *The Dream Songs*, taken from Olive Schreiner's *The Story of An African Farm* (1883): "But there is another method." This line was thrilling to me. It suggested another method of being, which I would later aim to embody in Ann-Marie's wilful anarchy. But it also suggested the principle of writing fiction itself. To write in a different way, to express what is true about female experience, but is more often never articulated. I found this principle in Gaitskill; I found it nowhere in mainstream culture.

Lauren Berlant has referred to "the female complaint" as "a space of disappointment, but not disenchantment." Conventional femininity means constantly refreshing one's faith in the power of salvation by love. Toward the end of "A Romantic Weekend," however, Beth's disappointment in her lover appears resolute: "His voice was high-pitched and stupidly aggressive, like some weird kid who would walk up to you on the street and offer to take care of your sexual needs. How, she thought miserably, could she have mistaken this hostile moron for the dark, brooding hero who would crush her like an insect and then talk about life and art?"

Beth's desire to be crushed like an insect is thwarted by the amateurism of her lover's sadism. She is disappointed in his ability to dominate her. She is not disenchanted. De Beauvoir writes in "The Woman in Love" chapter of *The Second Sex*: "It is a searing disappointment to the woman to discover the faults, the mediocrity of her idol . . . Between the superhuman and the inhuman, is there no place for the human?"

It seems that inequality serves to dehumanize men as much as women, rendering both performers of cartoonish ideas of what gender, and indeed passion, consists. This is made clear as Beth's and her lover's attempts at violent sex disintegrate into a paranoid stillness: "They froze in their positions, staring at each other." If idolatrous love depends on the other's absence, then this moment of pure presence is alarming. Beth appears to be coming into consciousness of her abject state, perhaps even glimpsing a way out of it.

But in the car on the way back to New York, "she said that when she had taken LSD, she had often lost her sense of identity so completely that she didn't recognize herself in the mirror. This pathetic statement brought back her attractiveness in a terrific rush." For her, time takes on a "a grainy, dreamy aspect"; the car becomes a cocoon.

He tells her she's not really a masochist: "You might have fantasies, but I don't think you have any concept of a real slave mentality. You have too much ego to be part of another person." To which she replies, "Alright, I'm not a slave. With me it's more a matter of love." Gaitskill writes: "She was just barely aware that she was pitching her voice higher and softer than it was naturally, so that she sounded like a cartoon girl." Beth says: "It's like the highest form of love."

Rereading this story, I was profoundly disturbed by the ending. Like the people who search the walls for imaginary doors in the first chapter of Duras' *The Ravishing of Lol Stein*, or Lol herself, who hurls her body against a locked door under the delusion that it is open, Beth condemns herself to yet another loop of self-abasement. Her masochism renews itself with a momentum that seems hypnotic.

In the words of de Beauvoir, she is "duped by mirage." The sparkling vision of love which Beth erects as a barricade against reality is an instance of existential bad faith, a means to abdicate from the difficulties of freedom. It is a paradise of enchantment, but one that leads to death in life. Her wish to be a slave to love is "really cute," her lover thinks. "Sure it was nauseating, but it was feminine in a radio song kind of way."

ZOE PILGER is the author of *Eat My Heart Out*, which was published in the UK in 2014 and will be published by the Feminist Press in 2015. She is an art critic for *The Independent*, winner of the 2011 Frieze Writers Prize, and is working on a PhD at Goldsmiths, University of London.

KATE ZAMBRENO

on

KATHY ACKER

NEW YORK CITY, SUMMER 2013

Ever since I moved here a few months ago I have been walking around looking for ghosts. I have been craving an older, more excessive city. Something raw and broken and feral. Nan Goldin's girls with their tears and pubic hair. Peter Hujar's drag queens. Lydia Lunch ranting at the Pyramid Club.

Is it possible to mourn a city and time I never knew? I try to walk around Alphabet City—how literary that sounds. I think of everything written here. Wild women like Cookie Mueller in the East Village. A young Kathy Acker walking around like a punk Edie Sedgwick bankrolled by Sol LeWitt. All the brilliant free spirits, are they all dead?

The week I got here I was asked to be on a panel on "literary bohemianism" with Katie Roiphe at McNally Jackson Bookstore. I said no.

The relationship of art to the market feels psychotic here. The conversations about writing are conversations about publishing.

This city makes me feel psychotic.

I think of Kathy Acker's letters to Susan Sontag in *Great Expectations*, struggling over publicity, how to survive as an artist in the city. I want to hold a séance with Kathy Acker.

•

DEAR KATHY,
Who wants to be famous? Not me. But that is what is expected here. Visibility, brand, platform (gross gross gross). How can a radical artist survive here? And stay feral? How can art be political in society? (Rimbaud).

DEAR KATHY,
I am experiencing career suicide ideation.

DEAR KATHY,
What defines the middlebrow to me is that it is absent of any anger, and by that I mean devoid of any politics. Why worry about the mainstream? Why can't we live and write in the margins? You write that the margin is a way to be marginalized, that's why you hate "experimental." I love that you hate. I love that you hate and that your works derive from such hate. I hate too.

DEAR KATHY,

How to avoid feeling sold? Because I want to be successful, I want to be a success. What I would do for success, to not feel like a failure all the time, but success, I think, comes at a price, perhaps one's integrity. Do you feel too that American publishing is interested in success, not failure? Failure, I find, is so much more interesting.

DEAR KATHY,

Why can't I just be a boy genius?

DEAR KATHY,

I don't think New York City will ever love me. I don't think I'll ever love New York City.

•

All summer I kept on thinking of one of Jenny Holzer's texts: "IN A DREAM YOU SAW A WAY TO SURVIVE AND YOU WERE FULL OF JOY."

Kathy Acker lived in the same building as Holzer.

"Who can think about art in this miserable city?" In *The Adult Life of Toulouse Lautrec* Kathy made the painter a horny, ugly, alienated girl. New York City is Montmartre.

Early on in the work there is an alive and raw quality, a psychotic feralness. But this feels like a shift from hackneyed copies and repetitions, of her early experiments where a girl finds herself in satire, pulp fiction, in juxtaposition with pornography. This is the movement when the "I" is and is not Kathy anymore. Raw and abject diary entries, yet filtered through art history and persona, destabilizing everything and giving it this A-effect.

"I'm a total hideous monster. I'm too ugly to go out in the world . . . I'm extremely paranoid. I don't want to see anyone. I'm another Paris art failure. I'm not even anonymous. All I want is to constantly fuck someone I love who loves me." She writes that "To survive in New York is to be a little like those hamsters on a wheel, the wheel turns faster and faster." This is why she left, moved to London. She didn't have to subsist on being a parasite or fame-whore (although she did that too).

New York is exhausting and weird. I walk around Soho and look at all the rich bitches who are glacial in the extreme heat, wearing long sleeves. I realize either they are aliens, or I am. What is it like to be so good-looking and gentrified?

Unprofessional notes from a book proposal I tried to write this summer: "I want to write about feeling dirty and sweaty and gross in public as a woman and writer, like a witch."

At Catherine Malandrino the mannequin in the window wears a long red gown. Little specks of red paint splatter her white face. Like Carrie at the prom. (Bleeding, bleeding, I am always bleeding.)

I've been making lists of how disgusting my body is. How chipped my black toenail polish is. How filthy it is underneath my fingernails. The little toilet-paper sculptures I pull out of my pubic hair.

Being groomed is impossible. I wonder if grooming is a desire to look simple and easy, to be easily read. I want a beautiful and perfect text like I want a beautiful and perfect body. I want to be seen as an intellectual woman, a serious writer, but here in this New York City marketplace I want to be slim, young, fashionable. I walk around and suck in my stomach and worry over my yellow teeth. The day my book receives a review in the *London Review of Books* I am obsessing over pictures someone put on Facebook from the night before. I am at a friend's reading in Bushwick, my arms look so white and gross in a tank top. (My mother and her slim muscular arms, pointing out how flabby I am.) Ugh.

I get my haircut like David Wojnarowicz's hollowed Rimbaud photograph. I go to a salon that all the other feminist writers on the Internet in New York City go to as well, run by a former riot grrrl, who is also a feminist writer on the Internet. My models for haircuts are often writers I want to emulate—like Ann Quin's lovely proud brunette head, or Gertrude Stein in Balmain, or wrinkly Samuel Beckett. These are often links I send to the photographer who needs to take my new author photo. I also send Robert Mapplethorpe photos of a young, feral Patti Smith, and photos of an older Patti Smith, and Hujar's Susan Sontag reclining on the bed. I feel that's the image I want to project—fierce and striking, maybe scary. Intelligent and severe but also light, pretty, witty (cute). I am not sure which self I am anymore. I want to be ugly and bold, and then I want to be pretty and young.

I want to look like an alien, I told the girl cutting my hair. Because that's how I've been feeling, like an alien. The salon does not take my picture against the wall and put it up on their blog, like they do another confessional feminist on the Internet, who is something of a celebrity, a slim pretty blond woman who knows how to pose for pictures. I have weird feelings about this other woman. She seems to encapsulate the New York City literary scene for me, online and in real life, whatever that is—witty, bitchy, a popularity contest.

Kathy again: "I don't know how to present my image properly. When I'm with people, I either act like a changing wishy-washy gook or like an aggressive leather bulldog."

I have been sending little emails to myself thinking about this essay and this summer.

In the subject head: Identity Crisis

In the body: What does that mean?

•

The summer before I had my picture taken by a ladyblog. I wore all black. The picture they chose was of me with my eyes closed. Otherwise you look so intense they said. At the New York City party to celebrate the pictures I didn't know what to wear. So I bought a pink dress. Like a cotton, pink day dress. I don't wear pink. Like the pink dress Villette buys.

Kathy Acker stares at us from those metallic, pastel Grove Press covers, so solidified as to be almost coherent, crimson-lipped, and peroxide-butched.

She subverted the self-portrait, destabilizing the "I."

I don't want to smile in my author photo. Because for a while I always smiled, and this was something I wanted to resist.

Why isn't she smiling? My students asked me of Frida Kahlo. Why isn't she smiling?

Kathy Acker was reading Frida Kahlo's biography on her deathbed.

I think of Kathy Acker like a Claude Cahun character—a gender-fucking, playful, subversive terrorist. She poses with her beautiful body, but her silhouette is not that of a Hollywood ingénue. Muscled, tattooed, spiky-haired. Claude Cahun with a shaved head dyed green who freaks the fuck out of André Breton. More of a revulsion. A castration.

Acker's project is one of hijacking literature, antagonizing memoir.

What is confessionalism? As if there is a unified, coherent self. Kathy Acker manipulated this fiction. The author dies—*la petit mort*. Her personas are the literary equivalent of Cindy Sherman's iconography. Can we contain all of these selves? Who is "I"? I can be the sum part of literature and history. I can insert myself inside.

•

In my early twenties I wrote a column for an alt-weekly in Chicago under the pseudonym Janey Smith (after Acker)—a quasi-Proustian fuck list, not bringing in anything too illicit. (Can the fuck list be literature?) How shall I read this now, how to survey my archives of the self with compassion?

The texts of Kathy Acker expand beyond *It Happened to Me*, whether therapeutic-confessional or salacious-confessional within media culture, where girls are posed naked and then set on fire. The confessional as commodity wrapped up in being a coliseum—Kathy Acker torched this whole concept.

She wrote the self but her works were not *about* the self. She cast herself into a greater more expansive history and literature. To write *against* one's commodity status. She is writing the Young Girl far before. Except hers might be banal and entranced with her own image, she might have love stories, she might know her photo, but she is not a model citizen.

The younger woman writer is promoted almost exclusively by image. This is pernicious. Kathy took this concept and subverted it. She is not a readable, easy image.

Kathy was image, fame-whore, performance artist—but then her texts are wild experiments that fuck with all of that. The texts are bombs. Acker refused to be invisible, yet she disappeared within her works, she fragmented.

This is the compelling distinction. She presented a provocative, even scary image, refusing to be erased, but her texts were about anonymity and disappearance.

Her work was a manifesto, a manifesto for a writing and performance through and against shame and invisibility, gobbling up texts and vomiting them out, being a monster,

Mary Shelley as an eighteen-year-old girl terrorist. She satirized herself, made herself a grotesque, her Janey Smith, her alter ego, exorcising her past girlhood.

•

The very moment I turned the page to "Hello I'm Erica Jong" in my *Essential Acker* book, Elizabeth Wurtzel walked into the West Village Think Coffee with her black dog. A wraith out of this essay-in-progress. A female horror. Her thin leopard scrunchie, the shiny face, the harsh blonde. She ate a sandwich wrapped in plastic and looked at her phone. Her pose bent over. And I realized she is one of my wounded monsters.

As am I. My nose dripping, I keep the crumpled dirty tissues in my purse like my mother did. The next day I am back at the same coffee shop, sobbing in public, wounded over a recently ended intellectual and emotional love affair with a male novelist that turned suddenly abject. Wondering how I am going to survive as a writer, whether I'll ever be considered outside of the box of Angry Woman Writer.

I am weary thinking that my life as a writer would be to continue cannibalizing myself, being public. I've begun to question myself—what is self-promotion and what is inquiry, connecting the self to something larger? The lines, for me, have become blurred.

I know it's not fair to judge the pretty, white, confessional women who get put into dumb commodity boxes, posing lying down with outfits with price tags on them. I realize I would not want their level of visibility. That that kind of visibility, predicated on image, also comes with a price tag. I have been thinking about that cycle—the diaristic women writers who achieve attention, are unfailingly young, pretty, and white. Their confessions and images are seen as able to be sold, but then they are also taken down in public (on the Internet). Capitalism is still intensely gendered and women writers are still expected to be commodities—acquiescent, good citizens.

There is something unthreatening about the confessions of a white, pretty girl and her sex life. Even if she takes revenge, by telling her story, it does not ultimately threaten the order of things. She can still be put in her place—she is gleefully vivisected online. Fury, though, is another thing. Kathy's girls are passive and want to be fucked and want to be loved. Yet Kathy makes it threatening because she makes it grotesque. Her porn texts are too prickly to jack off to without feeling the threat of castration. The whole body of work reads like an act of gleeful revenge. Because it destabilizes the narrative of confessionalism, which functions as a sort of discipline. To confess one's sexuality is to feel and perform shame before an either dismissive or (falsely) redeeming public.

I write in my notebook: Elizabeth Wurtzel vs. Kathy Acker?

The difference is maybe ugliness. An awareness of vanity and horror. I mean, I don't know.

•

A good girl named Karen Lehmann shed her skin and became Kathy Acker (Acker, her married name). She shed that skin again to dissolve and fragment.

She is Karen or Kathy like I am Katie or Kate. We have good-girl names.

All the Karen Lehmanns I google:
Karen Lehmann is a wedding photographer in North Carolina.
Karen Lehmann is a librarian in Iowa.
Karen Lehmann is a real estate agent in Florida.
Karen Lehmann is an ear, nose, and throat surgeon in South Africa.
Karen Lehmann from New York City married a lawyer and announced it in the *New York Times* wedding section.

I realize that my writing is about conjuring up and murdering the girl I was and have allowed myself to become—a tender horror. I channel my past self into all of these blonde, toxic girls. An "I" that is not only about my past but also about my present self, still gagging on all of my contradictions. Marguerite Duras with her ravaged face and whisky, calling back to the girl she was. Clarice Lispector writing her monster, the abject girl in the markets at São Paolo while dying of cancer, her marvelous Marlene Dietrich face. Lispector, who writes in *The Hour of the Star*: "Am I a monster or is this what it means to be a person?"

Kathy Acker's girls are abject, stupid, fools (dogs) for love, forced into humiliating roles within capitalism. Lousy, mindless salesgirls, strippers, daughters in love with fathers. They are not empowered. But she is not (just) (directly) documenting masochism or abjection or a double bind, I don't think. This is not transcription. It's alienation. It's depersonalizing the concept of confessionalism and the self. It doesn't offer itself up to be easily consumed. It is also placing the self against a larger culture (and yet I love the diarists too, those who are writing about their experiences with direct feeling, I just feel that Kathy's project is incredibly brave and, more importantly, dangerous).

Romance narratives that colonize our brains, she made into campy soap opera. Like the opening of *Blood and Guts in High School*, my first introduction to Acker. Janey Smith is in love with her father. Later Janey is the dog trailing after a cruel Genet. Fucking the ambivalent father (Genet, Sade, Bataille, who don't love me either). Of *Blood and Guts* she said, "I wanted to take the patriarchy and kill the father on every level."

The contemporary consciousness is not a stream. It is jarring, fictive, evasive, colonized by other fictions and narratives.

I love the artists who portray the girl as a potential terrorist but who view this skeptically, from a loving yet sometimes satirical distance, who understand her indoctrination too into passivity, her ambivalent libertinism—Elfriede Jelinek, Vera Chytilová, Marguerite Duras, Kathy Acker. Rimbaud said he wanted to make his self the experiment and experience the poison.

Kathy Acker is not insincere—sometimes she taps into a vein of deep feeling.

She's conceptual but not bloodless. Totally impure.

•

Anne Carson said of Francis Bacon, that with his paintings, his portraits of viscera and horror, he removed a boundary. This is what Kathy Acker did too. Lately I have been thinking of a writer's career like a museum retrospective. I love retrospectives, how you realize an artist can go into the next room, and radicalize everything—the moment Louise Bourgeois began making her Cells, her memory rooms. When Kathy Acker began inserting herself inside literature. Her *cuntslerromans*.

In the desire to push myself, to radicalize, I look to Kathy.

My favorite models of the writer are possessed. The ones who speak to voices in a room. Lately I have been thinking of writing as a visitation. Genet nailing criminals to the wall. Kathy in a form of drag.
When one gets crazy and risky, perhaps beautiful things can happen. Can one push against an internalized conservatism?

In an interview with Sylvère Lotringer (one of Kathy's ex-lovers), Julia Kristeva speaks of Célinè's "opera of the flood"—the emotions, mess, the rhythm and force of it. And how it takes from an aesthetic based on the borderline. She talks about borderline patients, "the extreme fragility of their boundaries, the lie of the unified self, the fiction that therapy maintain that this is possible."

The oozy borderline sorts, who go back and forth from publicity to withdrawal.

I have taken to wearing too much makeup, old-lady makeup. Penciled red lips, Chanel red, penciled-in brows, black eye-liner. Sometimes I feel this is a sign of deteriorating health—that textbook I read on BPD. To be the disliked, strange, eccentric bag lady under the medical gaze.

Sometimes I feel skinless, raw, like I don't have a face. How can I be sure that I have any coherence unless I outline it?

This is how I've figured out the Internet. Once in a while when I'm feeling particularly fragile I'll binge on googling myself. But to practice self-care I'll avoid combinations like "Kate Zambreno," and "I hate," things like that.

Then I go on Twitter and Facebook approximately five hundred times until I feel sick and crazy.

When I binge online I feel paranoid, fearful, weird, itchy, unhealthy, unsafe, stressed.

The paranoia of a girl or woman in public. The grotesque.

This psychosis triggered on or by the Internet, our repository of confessions. Fernando Pessoa's heteronyms and Kathy Acker's personas, the contemporary condition. This online fragmentation.

I would have loved to have witnessed Kathy Acker terrorize the Internet.

Would a commercial publisher take a chance on Kathy Acker's writing now? I think they would say her works are too unfinished, violent, porny, queer, risky, litigious. They would say "too unreadable." "This is not what the reader wants." And Kathy says, "I could give a fuck about what the reader wants." Her work is not based in the continuous character or narrative.

The promise of success and being self-congratulatory is so seductive—to turn in bourgeois narratives that prey on identification. Thomas Bernhard the Great Viennese Hater flips this, and makes his characters total frauds. Kathy Acker, our Great American Hater, makes them fictions.

There needs to be a word for the parasitism of middlebrow art and literature that steals from interesting and radical art but in the process strips it of its ferality, its political urgency, its threat. (Sarah Schulman uses the term "gentrified," also connecting it to Acker.)

> DEAR KATHY,
> How can I plot to throw a bomb in the face of my possible success, which I do not want? Then someone will ask, then why does she publish? As a great act of revenge against the culture.

Kathy antagonized the commercial mindset. And she is still so often misread, mischaracterized, her radical, ragey politics stripped away, seen as a trick or stylistic pyrotechnics that can be easily imitated. That is not to say her works are not readable, which is often what I'm told. Her works are not easy. Because they are not meant to be easily consumed or simply titillating. None of her books need to be finished. They deal with what Sianne Ngai has called "ugly feelings." Her work engages in tedium, annoyance, revulsion, titillation, confusion, similar to the "selective inattention" of witnessing avant-garde theater.

There is no room for decorum within a Kathy Acker text. She takes the brutal flood of sex and violence in Guyotat and further dismays it. Not only copies it, destabilizing the reader, she creates a fuck funhouse where she jerks you around after jerking you off. This is not often a pleasant experience. That's why Kathy belongs in the realm of the writing of cruelty, Artaud's daughters of the cunt. Kathy in an interview: "I want to say 'fuck, shit, prick.' That's my way of talking, that's my way of saying 'I hate you.'" The opera of the flood.

A great artist is not meant to be consumed, but to devour.

This work is terrorism against the body of white male literature. Writing against and appropriating and inserting herself into Great Male Texts. Taking on the role of the hysteric, the mimic, like Irigaray. Acker was a voracious reader, after Barthes. She is Pip in *Great Expectations*. She is Don Quixote, the knight having an abortion, trying to awaken as a great artist. At the opening of *Don Quixote* the green paper of the hospital gown turns into writing paper. Writing the body. Writing sickness. Janey Smith walking around with pelvic inflammatory disease.

DEAR KATHY,

Like David Wojnarowicz you have contracted a diseased society. You and David make an argument of the political necessity of writing about the sick body, to counteract silencing. Anyone who depoliticizes you has misread you.

DEAR KATHY,

I know I should wait until I'm like sixty to reject and radicalize my youth in writing, but what if I never make it to then? That's what I keep thinking. It feels inevitable to die of cancer of the lady parts. I think of your works' urgency, how you kept writing books. You knew you were finished with one project when you got bored. These games you played, casting yourself in the canon. I think of all of them, like Thomas Bernhard's oeuvre, as one book, punctuated by covers bearing your face.

DEAR KATHY,

David died and you died and one needs to make work of great risk and threat and vulnerability just as one needs to expose oneself to great risk and threat and vulnerability because you will die. Otherwise you will die. But you left behind a body of work—such a grotesque, beautiful, glittering body. An infuriating body, a provocative body. A body that raged.

DEAR KATHY,

I dream of you and you are devouring. I mix you up with my mother. My mother who died of cancer. Your mother's suicide. Our increasing demonologies like someone out of an Anna Kavan story. I think of you like my mother, mysterious and hard-nailed, evading with lies and myths. You are as slippery as she is.

DEAR KATHY,

You would tell your writing students to write about having sex with your weirdest family member. I feel with you an Oedipal-edible. I think the intimacy I feel for you would not have been reciprocated in real life. But it is an intimacy, a connection, that I need desperately. And the way you lived for writing, and reading, and wrote for me and girls and women like me.

DEAR KATHY,

I love Dodie Bellamy's description in her essay on your clothes, how you weren't friends but were suspended in mutual admiration and respect. (Love, on Dodie's side.) How, when Dodie once passed you at a party or reading she had a moment of knowledge that intimacy would be impossible for you two. That you would devour each other.

DEAR KATHY,

I want to write book after book of repulsive women.

DEAR KATHY,

Women writers are monsters, aren't they? We are all so devouring. Women writers I now see and admire as fellow female monsters, prickly, wounded, devouring—I feel I can't get too close to. I've wanted them to mentor me. It's impossible, except on the page. They now want me to mother them. Yet I am an unfit mother. I am a barren womb. Don't approach me and say you want to read me—which is telling me you want to love me. I will devour you. I will fill your life with so many words until you have none.

DEAR KATHY,

Was it the same for you?

DEAR KATHY,

The prickliness I feel for my peers, a paranoia. I want their respect more than anything. The female monster writer. Maybe this is because we are denied crucial space in the culture. But you took up space. You never asked for permission.

DEAR KATHY,

You craved community too but always felt like an outsider.

DEAR KATHY,

I despair of online feminism. Literature is political, but it's not ideology. It can't follow a party line. I love you for your infuriating contradictions. Your *Vogue* Spice Girls interview, declaring the girl band the true feminists, as a way to provoke, just to piss off some feminists. Kathy, its reviews by other women that have hurt the most. I am my texts. My texts are not feminist, too feminist, too sickly, too passive, too in love with fashion, etc.

DEAR KATHY,

Matias Viegener told me something, when I called him to ask about the Spice Girls interview. He told me something Avital Ronell said about you. She said, Kathy isn't one writer. She's many writers. I think that's true. That's what I love about you. Your multitudes.

DEAR KATHY,

I have begun taking pictures of gorgeous old ladies on my iPhone. It's making me love New York. My jouissance would be getting inside the closet of old Manhattan ladies with their art bobs who bought 1980s Commes des Garçons. I think of you in your Gaultier with sweat stains. Oh I love grotesque and glittery witches. I want to become them. Fashion as a collection of excess. I look at pictures online of Rick

Owen's wife and muse, Michele Lamy. She reminds me of you, how you might be now. She draws black eyeliner on her forehead to center herself. I love decadent crones, psychotic crones, gorgeous crones, who don't give a fuck. That's who I want to be.

DEAR KATHY,
I'm glad I haven't met you. I can appreciate your texts. I can read them as sustenance, as encouragement. I don't feel weird or crazy you won't blurb my book, or act diva-like with me, or don't want to read with me. I'm sure you were sometimes dreadful, a monster, generous, complex. But I don't have to feel bitter or wounded or ignored. I can feel your work and influence. I can love you completely.

KATE ZAMBRENO is the author of the novels *O Fallen Angel* and *Green Girl*, as well as *Heroines*.

The Feminist Press promotes voices on the margins of dominant culture and publishes feminist works from around the world, inspiring personal transformation and social justice. We believe that books have the power to shift culture, and create a society free of violence, sexism, homophobia, racism, cis-supremacy, classism, sizeism, ableism, and other forms of dehumanization. Our books and programs engage, educate, and entertain.

See our complete list of books at
feministpress.org

THE FEMINIST PRESS
AT THE CITY UNIVERSITY OF NEW YORK
FEMINISTPRESS.ORG

10114 R